debbie travis'
decorating solutions

debbie travis' decorating solutions

MORE THAN 65 PAINT AND PLASTER
FINISHES FOR EVERY ROOM IN YOUR HOME

by DEBBIE TRAVIS *and* BARBARA DINGLE

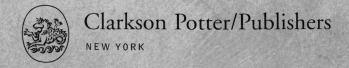

Clarkson Potter/Publishers

NEW YORK

TO THE WOMEN IN MY LIFE—

My granny, who taught me the art of storytelling;

My mother, for showing me that with hard work, imagination, and enthusiasm, you will succeed;

And my two sisters, for sharing the Travis sense of humor.

Copyright © 1999 by Debbie Travis

Photographs copyright © 1998 by the following: *Linda Corbett:* pages 46, 61, 111, 113, 115, 126, 135, 138, 146, 158, 162, 180; *Ernst Hellrung:* step-by-step photography as well as pages 18, 20, 21, 22, 23, 24, 26, 27, 28, 32, 65, 87, 88, 106, 152, 165, 176, 179; *Elaine Kilburn:* page 41; *Cookie Kinkead:* pages 43, 173; *Robert Pelletier:* pages 2, 8, 39, 42, 62, 66, 76; *Richard Poisson:* pages 44, 51, 52, 54, 59, 73, 74, 90, 94, 101, 102, 105, 116, 118, 119, 134, 142, 144, 154, 160, 161, 169, 175, 185; *George Ross:* cover shot and pages 11, 12, 34, 37, 38, 40, 49, 57, 68, 70, 78, 80, 82, 85, 93, 96, 98, 108, 121, 122, 125, 128, 130, 132, 140, 149, 151, 157, 167, 170, 182, 186, 188, 189; pages 45 and 110—photos courtesy of L.M. Scofield Company.

Photographs of Anaglypta and Lincrusta on Contents page and page 31 courtesy of Crown Decorative Products, Ltd.

Published by Clarkson Potter/Publishers, New York, New York.
Member of the Crown Publishing Group, a division of Random House, Inc.
www.crownpublishing.com

CLARKSON N. POTTER is a trademark and POTTER and colophon are registered trademarks of Random House, Inc.

Mylar is a registered trademark of E.L. Du Pont De Nemours & Co., Inc., U.S.A.

Printed in China

Design by Platinum Design, Inc. NYC

Library of Congress Cataloging-in-Publication Data
Travis, Debbie.
  [Decorating solutions]
  Debbie Travis' decorating solutions: more than 65 paint and plaster finishes for every room in your home / by Debbie Travis.
    p. cm.
  Includes index.
  1. House painting—Amateurs' manuals. 2. Texture painting—Amateurs' manuals. 3. Furniture paint-ing—Amateurs' manuals. 4. Interior decoration—Amateurs' manuals. I. Title.
  TT323.T72 1999
  698'.1—dc21
      98-19427

ISBN 1-4000-5263-7

10 9 8 7 6 5 4 3 2 1

First Edition

acknowledgments

Debbie Travis' Painted House started airing on television in 1995, and is now seen in over 50 countries. This is the second book inspired by the series. To create such a book takes months of painting, decorating, photographing, writing and editing, which all require a great deal of work, fresh ideas and most of all, devotion from an exceptional team. I would like to thank the following talented people who are not only my colleagues but also my friends.

ARTISTS

My immense gratitude goes to all the artists who have lent their talents: Alison Osborne, Bruce Emo, Pauline St-Amand, James Simon, Susan Pistawka, Andrejs Ritins, Anne Coté, Steve and Kelly Wilkie, and Ann Francis Oakes.

DESIGNERS

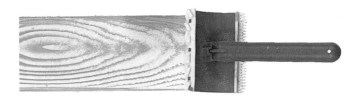

Many thanks to Valorie Finnie and Elaine Miller for their skills in begging and borrowing furnishings to make all the rooms in the book look so beautiful. Thanks to James Finnie, Susanne Van Lith, and Manuela Hunger for all their hard work behind the scenes. A huge thanks to Dana MacKimmie for her enormous repertoire of talents, whether with a paintbrush or a pen.

PHOTOGRAPHERS

All the stunning photography is thanks to the work of George Ross, Ernst Hellrung, Cookie Kinkead, Robert Pelletier, Linda Corbett, Elaine Kilburn, and Richard Poisson.

POTTER

Many thanks to Pam Krauss at Clarkson Potter for her faith in a second book, and to my editor, Margot Schupf, whose hard work, love of the job, and enthusiasm has pulled it off again. And to Kathleen Phelps and Jane Treuhaft for their expert eye in laying out the book.

TV NETWORKS

Special thanks to the Women's Television Network in Canada for their loyalty and support of the TV series, and to WGBH Boston and their Public Television Station colleagues in the United States and all the other TV Networks around the world who air *The Painted House.* An enormous thanks to all the viewers: this book is for you.

BARB

Most of all, I would like to thank and hug Barbara Dingle, who transfers my ideas and thoughts into the written word with patience and grace, often burning the midnight oil with ice packs on her wrists.

And finally, for my boys, Hans, Josh, and Max. It's all for you.

contents

introduction

JUST AS THE WINDOWS ARE THE EYES OF A HOUSE, THE WALLS, FLOORS, AND CEILINGS ARE THE SOUL. YOU DON'T NEED MUCH TO MAKE THEM BEAUTIFUL.

Decorating is an ongoing process. Each time you change your address, or even if you stay in the same place, the process of adapting your home to suit your changing moods and needs is constant, because, in truth, no room is perfect. It's either too big or too small, too modern for your taste or too old fashioned; the ceilings are too low or too high, and the floor is old or unfinished. Unless you have had the luxury of planning and building a new home from the bottom up—and maybe even then too—there will always be things about the design and colors you'll want to change.

However, when faced with a new set of walls, many of us are stumped. We look around a new home with large expanses of plain white walls or somebody else's color scheme, or an apartment that hasn't been painted in years, and we simply don't know where to start. I imagine that you, like me, wouldn't try to tackle the whole house or apartment at the same time. That could be overwhelming. Instead, you might have a general plan for the whole house but work on one room at a time. Decide what you like and don't like about the room, what its best features are and where the problems lie. It's important to focus on your living space and recognize the individual parts that make up the whole picture.

Take some time to think about your home's different features, the good and the bad, the walls, floors, and ceilings that compose each room. Make a list of what you love about your home—it could be as simple as a

pretty window that looks out onto a garden, or an impressive skyline, or interesting architectural details such as carved moldings or trim. Perhaps the floors are new or freshly refinished, or there's a fireplace perfectly situated in the family room. Small rooms or extra space under the stairs can also be special features, just the right size for a cozy study or intimate seating arrangement. Or maybe the kitchen is what sold you on the house, offering modern appliances and a clever layout that translates into less work for you.

Now go through your home, mentally or physically, and think about what bothers you the most. It could be as simple as changing the color of the walls, or it may go beyond that. What about the choice of building materials? Floors, doors, kitchens, and bathrooms may be serviceable but built with products like veneer paneling, plywood, and stock cabinetry that are economical but don't suit your tastes. Pointy stucco ceilings are an all-too-common sight in new apartments and houses, and in older homes, and the rough texture of this stucco can be an eyesore. Anything in poor repair exudes an aura of neglect. Cracked walls, peeling paint or wallpaper, waterstained ceilings, wood floors, doors or trim that have split or splintered, and built up layers of dirt are negative features you will want to change.

Now that you have a good idea of what you have and what you like, as well as what you'd rather not see, you've reached your starting point in the decorating

OPPOSITE: *The frescoed walls in this hallway—even though reminiscent of a different time period—complement the Victorian architecture.*

9

process. In order to be happy with your surroundings, the solution (short of extensive remodeling) is to accentuate the positive and camouflage or at least diminish the negatives with your decorating choices. Most of us use these two methods when we decorate, as it's not feasible to change everything at once, and if you're renting some things can't be changed at all. The combination works every time.

If you have a home, you have walls, and whether they're high or low, they are a canvas to dress up any room. Tall walls imbue a room with the airy, luxurious feeling of open space. If you're fortunate enough to have high ceilings, make the most of a good thing. If you have a small room with ordinary furniture, make the walls an interesting design and that is what people will see. Weathered wallboards and stenciled wall paneling would suit old boards in a country home. Attic rooms take their shape and personality from the slope of the roof—to emphasize the charming curve of an unorthodox meeting of ceiling and wall, nothing compares to a painted border. Hardwood floors in good condition are magnificent: a simple high gloss varnish will intensify the wood's rich tones and graining so that they shine during the day and give off a soft gleam at night. There are many ways to enhance specific features that you love.

Paint is an incredibly versatile decorating tool. Because you can paint over virtually any surface, you have the power to change the look of any room simply by adding a coat or two of paint. Painted finishes do a remarkable job of covering up uneven or less than perfect surfaces.

When you're faced with out of date or run-down kitchens or bathrooms and costly replacements have to wait, use paint to create a diversion with a lively backsplash to diminish the effect of a stained or cracked counter; apply a wall finish with life and luster to offset the color of yesterday's ho-hum bathroom tiles. Transform building materials such as wood veneer, plywood,

or laminate with a layer of paint or stenciled and stamped motifs. Unattractive floors can be enlivened with simple stains, geometric stenciled designs or other patterns. Break up a large unbroken expanse of wall space with a decorative panel or dado. By applying different blocks or sections of color to a wall surface, you can effectively reshape any space to suit your needs. A fireplace is usually the focal point of any room, and there are numerous ways to dress it up to suit your space. Change the look with paint alone, or by building detail with fiberboard and trim and then adding a finish that imitates real stone, metal or tilework.

As we experiment with new finishes, we also re-examine and reinvent solutions that were popular centuries ago. Along with the many paint finishes made easy in this book, I'm going to show you some of the newest and hottest looks today with painted plaster. Tinted plaster is as easy to apply as paint, covers up a myriad of sins, and is a wonderful tool for adding durable color to your walls. Also, two wall coverings that made their debut one hundred years ago in England make a stunning addition to any collection of decorative solutions. Lincrusta and Anaglypta are materials that are meant to be painted and look fabulous with a blended paint effect or metallic paint finish rubbed over their embossed designs.

I've gathered together my best ideas and divided them into problem-solving categories. Although we show how most finishes can be applied to one or two specific areas, almost any finish can be used elsewhere to great effect. For example, Anaglypta can be used as a backsplash as well as a dado; faux marble can be used as a floor border and also on furniture. Once you've used a few of these solutions to solve your own decorating dilemmas, you'll see how exciting and easy it is to create your own personal style. Then you can experiment with confidence.

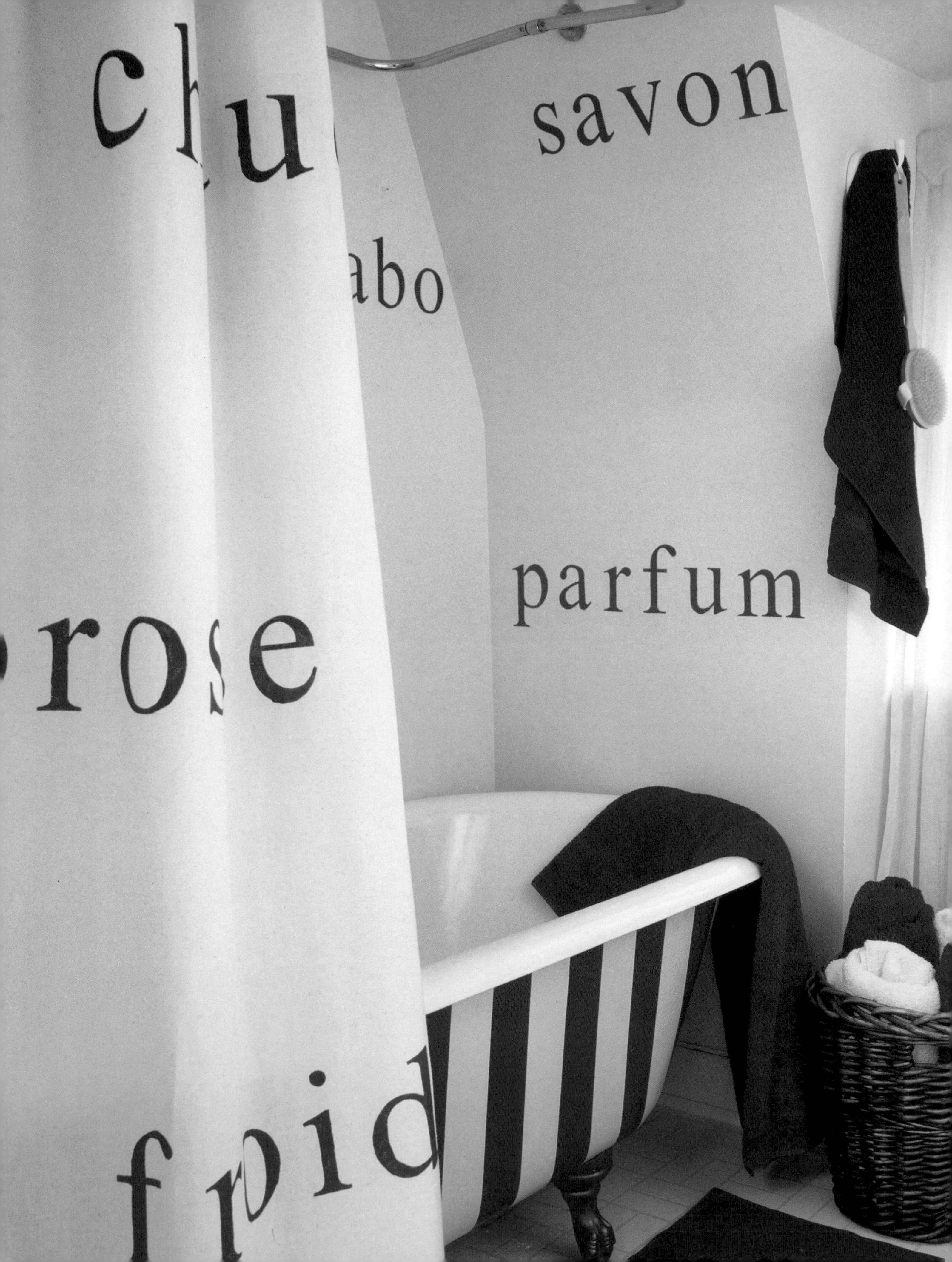
savon
parfum
rose

before I start painting

Taking the decorating plunge is very exciting. It's amazing what a burst of energy you get once you have decided to make a change and have formed a picture in your mind of just how your new room is going to look. It's tempting at this stage to skip the preparation and concentrate solely on applying that wonderful new finish. But most surfaces require some work before they're recovered, and if you neglect these important steps, you will inevitably be disappointed with the final outcome. It's also easier to apply a new painted or plastered finish to a well-prepared surface. The results speak for themselves.

OPPOSITE: *We've painted everything in this charming Victorian bathroom—even the claw-footed bathtub. Just make sure the sides of the tub are properly cleaned and primed if you want to do the same.*

preparation and tools of the trade

The projects in this book deal mainly with water-based paint and glazes, but I have incorporated some new products that make a wonderful complement to paint. Plaster has an inherent durability and fine texture that make it an inspiring medium. And two embossed wall coverings, Lincrusta and Anaglypta, present a remarkable background for tinted borders and dados.

These materials and the tools required to apply them are described in the following section. Once you become familiar with the wide variety of resources and how easy it is to work with them, you can use any of the finishes in this book to answer your decorating needs.

Surface Preparation

Preparing a surface for paint ensures that the paint will adhere to that surface. Paint will not stick to dirt, grease, or a shiny finish. It's important to follow the preparation guidelines specific to each material: for example, walls may be new or old plaster, drywall, wood, or wood veneer; floors may be wood planks, parquet, plywood, or linoleum.

The first step is to clean away any dirt and grease. Next, you should repair cracks and holes. Then sanding, which has a dual purpose: it removes small bumps and evens out the surface around repairs, and it roughs up shiny surfaces so primers will adhere. Finally, you will need to apply a primer, then the base coat.

The instructions for most of the projects in this book begin after the base coat has been applied. Always follow the correct preparation steps before you proceed with the decorative finish.

Tips and Tools for Painted Finishes

Paint is the most versatile decorating tool we have. Available in hundreds of colors, it's inexpensive and easy to apply. There are so many different paint products on the market today that selecting one can be confusing, so I have given you a quick breakdown of the ones most commonly used. For each finish in the book, I've specified exactly what type of paint to use.

PAINTS AND GLAZES

LATEX, ACRYLIC, AND ALKYD PAINT

The paints you see at the paint store fall into three categories: latex, acrylic (water-based), and alkyd (oil-based). Although both latex and acrylic paint are water based, there are more acrylic resins in acrylic paint than in latex paint, which makes it more durable and slightly more expensive. For all the painted finishes in this book, ordinary latex paint is fine, but you might want to consider using acrylic paint in a kitchen or a bathroom because it is more durable in those areas. Latex and acrylic paints are more environmentally friendly than oil-based paint, because tools can be cleaned with soap and water and the paint can be thinned with water. Although latex and acrylic paints are both water based, they have different chemistries. Do not combine them.

Alkyd paint is used far less now that more environmentally friendly products are widely available. Due to the oil in it, alkyd covers a surface beautifully and smoothly but requires a long drying time. It requires mineral spirits for cleanup and for thinning.

NEW DRYWALL

1. Dust.
2. Add a skim coat of plaster if you want a very smooth finish.
3. If the drywall is not treated, prime it with water-based primer or shellac.
4. Sand if the surface is not smooth (for example, if the drywall paper is furry from oversanding the seams before you primed the wall).

NEW PLASTER (NEW WALLS, MOLDINGS, OR CEILING MEDALLIONS)

1. Fresh plaster must be allowed to cure (dry thoroughly) before you seal and finish it. This takes anywhere from 7 to 30 days, depending on the heat and humidity.
2. Sand, then dust gently, being careful not to scratch the surface.
3. If repairs are needed, use plaster of paris or caulk.
4. Seal with shellac or primer.

PLASTER AND DRYWALL THAT HAVE BEEN PREVIOUSLY PAINTED

1. Clean with water and detergent and let dry thoroughly, 1 to 2 days.
2. Repair cracks and holes with caulk.
3. Sand smooth.
4. If the previous finish was glossy, sand to break up the shiny surface.
5. If you are covering a dark color, apply a prime coat before the base coat.
6. Prime any repair work.
7. If the old paint is flaking, strip, sand, and prime the surface.

STUCCO (TREAT AS YOU WOULD PLASTER)

For rough stucco, like a pointy stucco ceiling, clean with a soft brush.

RAW WOOD (PANELING, DOORS, TRIM, FLOORS)

1. Dust, then wipe clean.
2. If you want the wood to remain porous so it will take a stain or a paint wash evenly, sand with a rough-grade paper. The milling process closes the pores; sanding reopens them.
3. Seal knots with shellac; the knots in pine will show through layers of paint after a year.
4. If you are painting to cover the wood, prime with shellac or oil-based or water-based primer. (Water-based primer will raise the wood grain.)
5. Sand the prime coat.
6. For a very smooth surface, skim-coat with wood filler to fill in the ridges, then sand again (not recommended for floors).
7. Dust, then wipe clean.

PAINTED WOOD

1. Scrape away any loose dirt.
2. Clean the surface with water and detergent and let dry.
3. Repair with wood filler or caulk.
4. Sand, then wipe clean.
5. Priming is not necessary unless you are changing from an oil-based to a water-based paint or are covering repairs.

PLYWOOD

1. Prepare as you would raw wood.
2. The seams between sheets of plywood must be caulked, sanded as smooth as possible so the seams don't show through the paint, and primed.

WOOD VENEER WALL PANELS OR CABINETS

1. Dust, then wipe clean.
2. Repair with wood filler.
3. Sand lightly.
4. Prime with water-based or oil-based primer.

PAPER VENEER WALL PANELS

1. Dust, then wipe clean.
2. Don't sand; it will scar or remove the paper.
3. Prime with oil-based primer (water-based primer could cause the paper to lift off).

LINOLEUM FLOORS, LAMINATES ON KITCHEN CUPBOARDS

1. Clean with strong detergent, then rinse and wipe dry.
2. Sand to rough up the surface.
3. Use special high adhesive or primer designed for shiny surfaces.

CEMENT FLOORS (BASEMENT, BALCONY)

1. Do not attempt to paint over a basement or ground-level cement floor where dampness is a problem; the water moving up through the cement will lift the paint.
2. Sweep, then wipe clean.
3. If not already sealed, prime with acrylic or oil-based primer.

CERAMIC WALL TILE

1. Clean thoroughly with detergent, including the grout.
2. Sand to rough up the surface.
3. Use primer made to adhere to shiny surfaces or specifically made to cover tile.

Any questions you may have about the chemical properties of paint can be answered at the paint store. But there is one golden rule to remember: You cannot apply a water-based paint or painted finish over an oil-based base coat, although you can apply oil-based paint over a water-based base coat. If you are unsure of the properties of your existing base coat, here is a simple test. Apply a 4-inch stroke of latex paint over the base coat and allow it to dry for 24 hours. Scrape at this paint; if it flakes easily, the base coat is oil based.

GLAZES

Most painted finishes are created by manipulating the paint once it is on the surface. Because the paint must remain slippery and wet long enough for you to play with it, a glazing liquid, or glaze coat, is mixed into the paint. The glazing liquid performs two jobs when mixed with paint: It makes the paint translucent, which allows some of the base-coat color to shine through, and it pro-

longs the drying time for painted finishes that depend on manipulating paint on or removing paint from the surface. Adding glaze to the paint won't change the true color of the paint, but because the glaze makes the paint translucent some of the base-coat color will shine through. These finishes are known as negative finishes. A positive finish is an effect such as sponging or stamping, in which the paint is applied directly to the surface with a tool. Glaze is not usually required for this.

Glazing liquid is available in a water-based form, which allows you to produce stunning painted finishes with latex paint. If you are using an oil-based paint, the glazing liquid must be oil based as well.

Some professionals roll on a coat of glazing liquid first, then apply and manipulate the paint over the glaze. I prefer to mix paint and glaze in a container first, then apply the colored glaze to the surface.

METALLIC PAINTS, POWDERS, AND LEAF

The lustrous qualities of bronze, aluminum, copper, silver, and gold are easily replicated with paint. Metallic paints come in three forms:

Metallic sprays are readily available in craft stores; some are water based and some are oil based, so read the label before you apply a top coat.

Metallic powders are the most popular way to make metallic paint. The powder is mixed directly into oil- or water-based products. For example, silver powder could be poured into gray paint for a silver finish. For a more translucent metallic finish, the metallic powder would be added to glazing liquid or varnish. You can do this yourself, or ask your paint store to prepare it for you. If you are making metallic paint from metallic powder, it is imperative that the surface be sealed with at least one coat of varnish when you are finished.

Note: Always wear a mask when working with metallic sprays or powders, because they become airborne and are toxic.

Gold and silver leaf. Real gold leaf is very expensive but will keep its luster for centuries. Most leaf used today is imitation. Because leaf is so thin and fragile, it is tricky to apply, so I recommend practicing first—the results are worth the trouble. To apply the leaf, a sizing medium is applied to your prepared surface; while the medium is still tacky, the leaf is laid down and gently patted into place. Transfer paper, while not as luminous as leaf, is less expensive and available by the roll, making it perfect for larger jobs.

PEARLESCENT PAINT AND POWDERS

These products add a shimmery, luminous quality to a finish that replicates qualities found in mother-of-pearl.

Always remember to wear a mask when you are handling powders.

CERAMIC PAINT (PORCELAIN PAINT)

This paint is designed to go directly onto shiny surfaces such as china, ceramic tile, glass, and terra-cotta. It is water based and comes in opaque and translucent forms. Ceramic paints must be heat set, either in a potter's kiln or a kitchen oven. Read the manufacturer's label for instructions, as brands vary.

COLORANTS

For most painted finishes in this book, I have mixed commercial latex paint with water-based glazing liquid. But there are times when purer colors are called for or when you may wish to custom-mix your own color.

Here are some of the most common colorants:

ARTISTS' ACRYLICS

These paints are what artists who are working in water-based products use to paint a canvas. Available at art and craft stores in tubes and plastic bottles, artists' acrylics come in a wide range of pure colors, and they are water soluble and fairly quick drying. They may be added to water-based paint or directly to the glazing liquid; only a small amount is required. I use artists' acrylics when a specific color is desired that is difficult to find among commercial paints, such as the earth tones of raw sienna, raw umber, burnt sienna, and burnt umber, to name a few. Adding them to a glazing

METALLIC PAINTS AND POWDERS

1. metal leaf
2. metallic spray paint
3. metallic paint
4. metallic powders
5. transfer foil
6. pearlescent paint

COLORANTS

1. artist's oil

2. artist's acrylic

3. universal tint

4. powder pigment

5. metallic powder

1.   2.   3.   4.   5.

liquid (you need to mix well) produces vibrant colors. If the ratio of pigment to paint or glaze is too high, the mixture's chemical properties will result in a poor finish. It's easier to buy commercial paint for dark colors.

UNIVERSAL TINTS

These are commercial liquid colors that paint stores add to paint to color or tint it. The tints are added to any type of paint or glaze, as well as varnish, stain, and plaster. This is usually how professional house painters color their paints. These tints cannot be applied to a surface in their pure form, because they have no dryers. Universal tints come in the primary colors and in earth tones; they are mixed together in specific sequences to produce the hundreds of colors you see on paint chips. A rudimentary knowledge of color theory and some experimentation are necessary to mix your own colors. Once you have the confidence to tint your own paint, you can save a great deal of time and expense. Universal tints are available in small tubes or large bottles at paint stores. Only a tiny amount is used, so take this into consideration when buying.

DRY POWDER PIGMENTS

Made from mineral or synthetic sources, these powder pigments are concentrated color that can be mixed into any liquid paint or glaze. The pigments are difficult to use without prior training. These pigments can be found in most art supply stores and produce fabulous colors ideal for colorwashing. Always wear a mask, because the powder is toxic.

ARTISTS' OILS

Artists' oils are used in the same way as artists' acrylics except that they are added to oil-based glazes. They come with the same advantages and disadvantages as oil paint.

SHEENS

Sheen plays a big part in the final outcome of a painted finish. The sheen, or gloss, on your surface will come from the final coat, whether it's paint, glaze, or varnish. Latex paint has approximately five different levels of gloss; varnish usually has three. Glazing liquid generally dries to a satin sheen.

Some painted finishes that call for a great deal of manipulation, such as faux marbling, require the slippery surface of a semigloss base coat. A satin or an eggshell sheen is best for mixing with glazes, for it adds just the right amount of reflective properties for most finishes and is somewhat slippery. A matte base coat absorbs the glaze and will speed up the drying time.

Applying two different sheens on a surface will produce its own pattern, because light will bounce off the higher sheen and be absorbed by the lower sheen. Unless you intend to use different sheens as part of an effect (as is done in shadow striping, where a high-sheen varnish is rolled in stripes over a low-sheen base coat, creating the appearance of two tones of the same color), don't mix sheens in the same project.

I rarely use high gloss unless I want a luxurious, shiny finish. To show the luster of faux marble, a mid sheen works well; for country-style effects, use a low sheen.

FLAT, OR MATTE

1. Provides a uniform finish, because it absorbs light and hides surface irregularities.
2. Used on ceilings and any areas that do not get touched.
3. Not very durable or easy to clean.

SATIN, EGGSHELL, OR VELVET

1. Provides a subtle, lustrous sheen.
2. Good for walls in living rooms and bedrooms; ideal for mixing with glazing liquid.
3. Easier to clean than flat or matte.

SEMI- OR MEDIUM GLOSS

1. Reflects light well; will play up surface irregularities such as drips, dents, and holes.
2. Very durable and easy to wipe clean.
3. Used on woodwork, trim, cabinets, and paneling.
4. Good for kitchens and bathrooms.
5. Slippery surface ideal as a base coat for painted finishes that require manipulation.

HIGH GLOSS

1. Highly reflective; magnifies surface flaws.
2. The most durable and easiest to clean of all sheens.
3. Used on doors and some trim.
4. Highly reflective quality provides necessary depth for certain finishes.

TOOLS FOR PAINTED FINISHES

Many tools are available that help you create textures and designs with paints and colored glazes. But there are many professional tools that can be replicated at home with inexpensive materials. Some of the most effective and sophisticated finishes, such as ragging and fresco, call for nothing more than a paintbrush and a rag. Other techniques are made more authentic with softening brushes (faux marble) or a rocker (wood graining).

If you have never tried a painted finish before, it's best to start with less elaborate tools. Once you're hooked, investing in a few professional tools will make your work easier and more enjoyable, and the results will be more satisfying.

Take good care of your tools and they will last a long time. Always clean brushes immediately, and with the appropriate cleanser: warm water and soap for washing out water-based products such as latex, acrylics, and glazes; mineral spirits and then soap and water for oil-based products. Shake out the drips and either lay flat or hang to dry completely. Wrap in brown paper to store.

REGULAR PAINTBRUSHES

These are the brushes most commonly seen at paint and hardware stores. Most of your painting can be done with them. The cheapest are not necessarily a good buy because the bristles fall out easily and will remain behind on your painted surface. Use synthetic bristles for latex paint, natural bristles for oil.

FOAM BRUSHES, OR SPONGE STICKS

These foam-tapered brushes come in a variety of sizes. They are inexpensive and disposable. Good for small jobs, they leave a smooth finish and no brush marks. They are not appropriate for applying paint or glaze over embossed surfaces; a bristle brush is required to get into the crevices. They are ideal for varnishing small surfaces such as furniture and even dados and panels as they do not leave brushstrokes.

1.   2.   3.   4.   5.   6.

SPECIALTY BRUSHES AND TOOLS

1. FITCHES AND ARTISTS' BRUSHES

These long-handled brushes come in a variety of shapes and sizes. The large round-ended and pointed ones are ideal for applying glazes to small areas such as dados and furniture. The smaller fitches are used for more intricate work.

Alternative: small standard paintbrushes and artists' brushes found in craft and hardware stores.

It's always useful to have a couple of artists' brushes for intricate work or for filling in mistakes. The cost varies greatly depending on quality. The most expensive are made from sable; the cheapest, found in paint stores, have synthetic bristles.

2. DRAGGING BRUSH

This long-haired, natural-bristle brush is used for dragging through a colored glaze to create bold brush strokes. A wide dragging brush is used to simulate the look of silk, known as strié. A dragging brush is also used in wood-graining techniques.

Alternative: any long-haired, thick-bristle (synthetic) brush.

3. BADGER HAIR SOFTENING BRUSH

These come in a variety of sizes. All are expensive, because they are made from real badger hair, but the soft blending effect they create is magical. They are used for softening the glazes in faux marble and many other finishes. Hold the dry brush loosely at a right angle to the surface and softly rub the glazes to blend them together.

Alternative: soft-bristle standard paintbrush.

4. FEATHER

Although there is a professional brush called a striper that creates the veins in faux marble, it is rarely used today. A feather does the ideal job.

5. STIPPLING BRUSH

This is a flat-ended brush in the shape of a brick with a solid wood handle. When the dry brush is softly pounded onto wet glaze, it creates a finish of fine dots. A professional stippling brush is expensive but takes far less time to cover a large wall surface. Stippling brushes come in many different sizes; the largest are quite heavy to work with.

Alternative: Thick, flat-ended, hard-bristle brush.

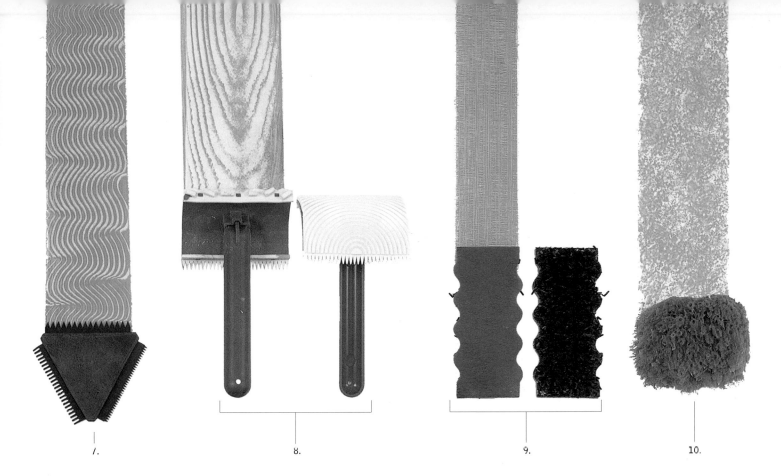

7.
8.
9.
10.

6. STENCIL BRUSHES

These are flat-ended round brushes that create tiny dots of paint when stippled onto a surface. They are ideal for stenciling: Little paint is used so that it does not leak underneath the stencil. These brushes range in size from ¼ inch to 3 inches in diameter.

7. RUBBER COMBS

Combs are traditionally used as wood-graining tools. Each side of the triangular comb has different-sized teeth that, when pulled through the glaze, create the markings found in different woods. Combs are also used to create a variety of patterns, depending on how they are pulled or waved through the glaze.

Alternative: You can cut out a custom comb from foam core. This enables you to design the size and spacing of the teeth and the overall size of the comb.

8. ROCKERS

Rockers are used to re-create the graining and knots typical of pine and are made from thick rubber that has been engraved with a grained pattern. You rock the tool back and forth as you pull it through the glaze, thus creating the pattern.

9. SPECKLE AND DRAGGING TOOL

A new tool on the market, this inexpensive plastic brush is available at some paint and hardware stores. Its twisted rubber base scratches through the wet glaze, leaving a fine weave effect. It is an ingenious little tool. I also call it a denim brush because I use it to re-create the rough weave of denim in some finishes.

Alternative: The working surface of a denim brush resembles the sharp fibers of a strip of Velcro, which when dragged through wet glaze re-creates the texture of linen or denim. If you can't find the tool, make your own by gluing rough-sided Velcro onto a wood block.

10. SEA SPONGES

These natural sponges are used to dab paint over a surface to create a finish of small, irregular dots and to blend colors together. Available at drugstores and paint stores.

Alternative: Cut up kitchen sponges and pull out bits of the edges to make the shape irregular. Because the surface of a kitchen sponge is flat, you won't get the same random impression as with a sea sponge.

1. homemade roller for specialty designs
2. long-handled sponge roller
3. foam roller
4. small thin pile roller
5. thick pile roller
6. small sponge roller
7. decorative molded rubber roller
8. homemade patterned foam roller
9. textured stucco roller
10. low pile rollers

ROLLERS

Rollers make quick work of applying paint or a colored glaze over a large, flat surface. A removable roller sleeve fits over a wire cage that is attached to a handle. The handles on some of the larger rollers are designed to take a pole extension for hard to reach areas, and there are long-handled rollers that fit behind radiators. There are a variety of roller sleeves available in foam, synthetic, or natural fibers. For rough surfaces such as stucco, use a split foam roller or a medium nap roller; a thin nap or foam roller is best for smooth surfaces, and when you are using water-based paint. Small foam rollers are ideal for furniture, or when you are practicing on a board.

There are rollers available that simulate the look of painted finishes such as ragging. Pieces of plastic attached to the sleeve flick the glazed surface as you roll. The result is more uniform than ragging, and lacks the subtle shading of a handpainted finish—it looks rather like wallpaper. It can be very messy as the paint has a tendency to spatter as you go, so protect the surrounding area—and yourself with drop cloths and work clothes.

Also, there are specialty rollers that have a design precut into a rubber sleeve. They work along the same lines as a rubber stamp, but applying a pattern with a roller is quicker. It does take some practice, however, and is not as forgiving. See Damask walls, page 68, to get an idea of what these look like.

As a creative alternative, you can make up your own design by cutting out shapes or remolding a foam roller. It's always fun to produce an imaginative custom finish. See Dotty Stairs on page 171, and the Plaid dado on page 87 for instructions.

Paint trays are necessary when using a roller, and plastic inserts are available for quick cleanup. The paint well can be divided into sections with cardboard and masking tape so that you can roll on two or more colors at a time.

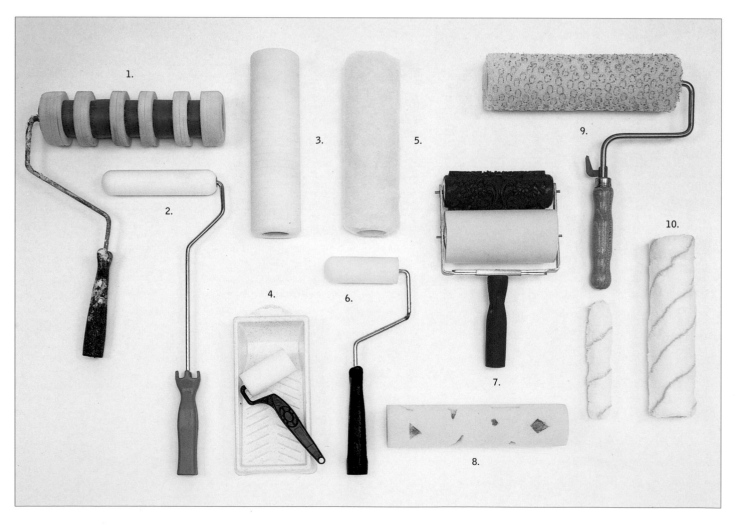

Tips and Tools for Stenciling

Enthusiasm for stenciling has grown to the point where stencils now often replace wallpaper borders as a finishing touch for a room. There are literally thousands of patterns sold in stores and through catalogs, so you should have no trouble finding a stencil to match your room decor.

Stencils come in numerous sizes and shapes and of varying quality. The best stencils have been laser cut from Mylar, a tough, clear plastic sheet that bends easily into and around corners.

Stenciling can be as easy as a simple motif on a chest of drawers or as complicated as a three- or four-layer pattern. The number of layers in a pattern is the number of times you will have to go around the room. I am a great fan of stencil designs that come in only one piece; now, with stencil creams, you can add the colors and shading all at once.

Stencils are not limited to the traditional vines and flowers. They also replicate architectural moldings and intricate patterns. Some companies will cut a stencil to a specific design; for example, they will take a swatch of fabric, trace a pattern from that, and cut it for you—or you can do this yourself.

You may be surprised at the cost of some stencils, but the most expensive designs are still less than wallpaper. And stencils can be used repeatedly. Perhaps you and a friend could go in together on one or two stencils and trade with each other. No two people will fill in a stencil in the same way.

Anyone can stencil. It's a technique that is quick and easy to learn. You can add more complex designs and details to your repertoire as you become more familiar with the tools and procedures. The main prerequisite is patience. If you try to rush and use too much paint on your brush at one time, it will leak under the stencil and ruin your design. You need to apply very little paint and build up the color. It is not meant to be heavy. If you have never stenciled before, you will be surprised at how little color you need to make an impact.

Unlike a painted finish, stenciling doesn't have to be done all at one time. You can leave your design whenever you want and return hours or days later.

Many mediums are used in stenciling. One of the

newest and most exciting is plaster, which produces not only the stenciled design but a three-dimensional look.

You may stencil over most surfaces, paint, and fabrics as long as they aren't too slippery. As with plain paint, stencil paints need something to grab onto for a lasting finish. Most stencils look better on a textured painted finish such as colorwashing or ragging. You can stencil over lightly textured stucco; the design will go nicely into the grooves and creases. But don't stencil a pattern over a busy finish such as faux marble.

You may use latex paint, especially if you are trying to match a paint color you have already used in the room, but be careful to apply it with a very dry brush. Be aware that latex will take longer to dry than stencil paint, causing a problem with repeat border patterns.

STENCILS

You may purchase precut stencils made from hard plastic, cardboard, metal, or Mylar. Or you may design and cut your own motif. Find or draw a design and use a photocopier to produce the size you require. Tape the photocopy to a cutting board, and lay a piece of Mylar

TOOLS FOR STENCILING

1. heat-cutting knife
2. X-acto knife
3. stencil brushes
4. stenciling paints
5. low-tack masking tape
6. cutting pad
7. precut stencil
8. carbon or transfer paper
9. Mylar
10. marker
11. spray glue

over it. Either trace directly onto the Mylar with a marking pen and then cut, or cut directly. Add holes or penmarks, called registration marks, at the sides or at the top and bottom. These are used to keep the pattern straight as you move along a border.

STENCIL PAINT

The paint used for stenciling is quick drying, which allows you to move the stencil along or add more than one shade quickly. Stencil paints come in different forms, all available at art and craft stores. There are acrylic stencil paints; Japan paints, which are oil based (but have a quick-drying agent added); and spray paint, which may be either water or oil based. Stencil creams or crayons are oil based and are dry to the touch immediately but take from 3 to 5 days to dry completely. The advantage of using them is they will not leak under your stencil, and the colors blend together beautifully.

If you are going to stencil on fabric, use paint especially designed for the job. Fabric paint is made to withstand washing and ironing.

BRUSHES AND OTHER TOOLS

Stencil brushes have stiff bristles and are round with a flat top. Small brushes are required to do intricate work such as vines or tiny flowers; larger brushes allow you to apply one color quickly over a pattern. You may use other tools to fill in stencils. Foam brushes, sponges, even rags will give the design their own special texture. Always be sure to apply just a little paint at a time to prevent leakage.

A heat-cutting knife can be used to cut stencils out of Mylar. This point gets extremely hot, so cut the Mylar over a piece of glass or heavy mirror: The heated point will burn through other surfaces.

STENCILING WITH LIQUID STENCIL PAINT (ACRYLIC, JAPAN, LATEX)

Note: The secret of good stenciling is to use as little paint as possible. Although it may seem that you are barely affecting the surface color, you will be surprised at the effect when the stencil is removed.

1. Position the stencil on the surface to be colored with small pieces of low-tack masking tape, or spray a small amount of spray adhesive on the back of the stencil. Make sure the stencil is face up.
2. Have paper towels or old newspapers on hand for removing excess paint from the brush.
3. Put a small amount of undiluted paint into a small container or a saucer. Use one container for each color.
4. Take a clean, dry stencil brush and dip just the tips of the bristles into the paint. Remove the excess paint onto the paper, using a circular motion so the paint becomes evenly distributed among the bristles.
5. Holding the brush like a pencil with the bristles flat on the surface, apply the paint to the cutout area using a stippling or circling motion. Build up the color to the required shade.
6. If a second color is required, keep the stencil in place and repeat with a new brush.
7. Carefully remove the stencil from the wall. Reposition the stencil to the left or right, lining up the registration marks or guidelines that you have marked.
8. Repeat until the border is complete.
9. If your stencil has several layers, stencil the whole area with the first stencil in the series, then repeat with the second, and so on.

STENCILING WITH STENCIL CREAM

1. Follow the procedure for positioning and moving the stencil as for liquid stencil paint.
2. Stencil creams come in little pots or sticks. Remove the skin from the surface of the cream or the top of the stick with a paper towel.
3. Take a clean, dry stencil brush and pick up some of the paint directly from the pot. Swirl the brush tips on a paper towel using a circular motion to distribute the paint evenly among the bristles. If using a stick, apply the paint onto an unused portion of the stencil first and then pick it up with the brush.
4. Apply the paint to the cutout area as for liquid paints.
5. Stencil creams are oil based. They dry to the touch immediately, but take 3 to 5 days to cure, or dry completely.

Spray paint is used for applying color to large areas. There is an art to applying color with a spray, because you cannot be very accurate when holding a can 12 inches away from the surface. The right touch is needed to apply the spray evenly, without drips. Always wear a mask because the paint becomes airborne and is toxic, and protect the walls, floor, and furnishings with newspaper and drop cloths.

Stamping and Block Painting

Stamping and block painting are the reverse of stenciling. Rather than filling in the cutouts of a stencil with color, you apply the color directly to the stamp, then press the impression onto your surface. The simplest stamping technique can transform a room with shots of color and character. A kitchen sponge cut to shape as a square or a triangle, then dipped in paint, is all you need to string a geometric border around a child's bedroom, or outline a series of doors or windows. You can stamp with anything around the house that has the shape you want—a bottle cork for dots or even the carved surface of a raw potato to create a faux leopard skin (see page 132). Stamping suits a plain painted background, but its naive style also works well over a colorwash and on wood.

For block painting, a pliable rubber stamp is used that has been precut into a specific shape, such as a leaf or a flower. It has a small handle, or tab, for you to hold when applying the paint and positioning the stamp. Block painting gives you more freedom than does a stencil to build up a design or a series of images in an artistic manner, because there is no preset map. Block painting has a whimsical quality that is embellished by

TOOLS FOR STAMPING AND BLOCK PRINTING

1. homemade sponge stamp
2. kitchen sponge
3. blocking glaze
4. block stamps
5. rubber stamps
6. X-acto knife
7. marker
8. kitchen sponge stamp

a background of broken color, such as ragging, fresco, or stucco. Latex paint may be used on its own, but the images will have a more translucent quality if you mix the paint with glaze.

There are block painting kits available that include the stamps, colored glazes, and complete instructions and pictures of the finished designs. But you can produce a custom version by cutting a stamp from a sheet of rubber and buying or mixing the glazes yourself.

INSTRUCTIONS FOR BLOCK PAINTING

1. Decide where you are going to put the design, and mark out some guidelines with a pencil.

2. Hold the rubber stamp by its tab. Using a ½″ brush, apply paint or colored glaze to the face of the stamp. You may use 1 color or add a little of 2 colors, but make sure the surface is covered completely up to the tab.

3. Holding the stamp by the tab, position the stamp on the surface, then press down with your fingertips on the back of the stamp. Lift the stamp, move it to a new spot, and print again. Print 3 or 4 times before adding more paint. Some prints may overlap if the design calls for it.

4. Use an artists' brush to make freehand designs if appropriate.

SEALANTS

1. foam roller
2. shellac
3. water-based varnish
4. oil-based varnish
5. professional varnishing brush
6. beeswax
7. foam brush

Sealants, Top Coats, and Wax

SEALANTS

Building materials that are porous, such as wood, dry-wall, and plaster need to be sealed before they are painted. Otherwise, the paint will continue to be absorbed into the wall or floor, and you will find yourself adding coat after coat of paint in an attempt to cover the surface. Painting wood can be especially challenging; it can take a few weeks or months before the natural resins seep through the paint layer, discoloring your work.

Paint primers do the job of sealing new materials as well as giving the surface the adhesive coat required for paint to stick. There are water-based, acrylic, and oil-based primers.

Shellac is an alcohol-based sealer that dries very quickly. It is excellent for sealing fresh plaster, drywall, and wood. However, the fumes are toxic, so wear a mask and work in a well-ventilated area.

TOP COATS

Many different names and products are used as a protective coating applied over paint: urethane, polyurethane, varnish, top coat, or clear coat. For consistency throughout the book, I have used the term *varnish*. The original oil-based variety has a yellow tint; it dries almost clear but yellows over time. This affects the colors underneath; you've no doubt heard of painted floors yellowing. There is no solution to this problem except to strip off the finish and repaint the floor. However, acrylic varnish makes it possible to apply a clear top coat that will not yellow. The varnish is water based, so it dries quickly, which is particularly important when three or four coats are necessary. And the acrylic resins make the varnish very durable.

Varnish comes in different sheens, which are important to consider because varnish is the last coat to go on. Refer to the section on sheen (page 18) for the various degrees of shine and for where each is suitable. High-sheen floors look spectacular, but they are more slippery than those with a matte sheen. Adding color to varnish

is a good way to give a subtle overall look to a freshly painted finish on walls or floors.

A protective top coat is necessary only for surfaces that get considerable wear and tear, specifically floors. I always recommend at least four coats of varnish for floors.

Painted finishes are inherently durable because the glazing liquid has protective properties in it, as do all of today's good-quality paints. You will not have to top-coat walls unless you have applied a colorwash of diluted paint and water only, in which case one coat of varnish is advisable in a kitchen or a bathroom.

WAX

Wax as a top coat can add a final touch of authenticity to your finish. A thin layer of beeswax rubbed over faux leather panels not only gives added protection but the sheen and feel of real animal hide. Waxes can be colored with powder pigments for antiquing moldings and trim. Carefully heat the wax until it is liquid enough to be mixed then add a small amount of pigment. Leave to cool and harden.

As a final step for Venetian plaster walls, a coat of wax may be applied and buffed to a glossy sheen.

You can also use wax as a speedy distressing technique, streaked between layers of paint. The top coat of paint will not stick to the wax and will lift off easily, revealing patches of the undercoat that would show through if the wood had aged naturally.

TOOLS FOR PLASTER FINISHES

1. bucket of water
2. universal tint
3. ornamental gesso
4. drywall compound
5. trowel
6. tinted Venetian plaster
7. plaster of paris
8. metal spatulas

Tips and Tools for Plastered Finishes

A NEW AGE FOR PLASTER

Plaster as a decorating tool is back. We have fallen in love with the weathered and aged plaster walls of antiquity and want to live with them in our homes. The mellow blending of earthy colors, gray, pink, and terracotta, as well as a cool, silky smooth touch are trademarks of a plastered surface that has been worn and polished by time and the elements.

Most of us think of plaster as a product for filling cracks, or the plaster used to construct lath and plaster walls, or as the stucco used on ceilings and fireplace surrounds. But today we have moved one step further in the decorative world of plaster. There are now many new and inventive ways of using plaster and stucco.

There are new products such as Venetian plaster that has a base of marble dust so that it can be burnished to a high sheen. Gesso, used by artists to smooth their canvases before painting, is now being employed to fill in a stencil design as an alternative to paint. And although this reinvented medium may seem intimidating to work with at first, some find it easier to apply than paint.

The longevity of color-blended plasterwork, such as magnificent Italian frescoes, is due to the method of applying color to the plaster while it was still wet. The color was absorbed into the plaster rather than being applied as just a surface coating and was therefore infinitely more durable than paint. Today, we have tinted-plaster products that accomplish the same feat in fewer steps. Just like paint, colored plaster can be mixed, then applied directly to the wall. As with paint, tinted plaster can be layered to create depth and character.

You may already have plaster walls or a plastered finish in your home. Builders in the 1940s and earlier constructed walls with plaster over lath. Plaster was commonly used in the 1960s and 1970s in the form of stucco around fireplaces and in basements and was usually painted white. Stucco is still commonly used on ceilings in a rather dreadful pointy, icing sugar texture that is meant to cover up flaws and to last a long time. Unfortunately, these ceilings are difficult to paint or repair.

Although many of us have a horror of these dated stucco effects, there are solutions to updating and improving their look. And painted stucco is actually making a huge comeback, although it is treated differently now. It's far more sophisticated and is an attractive alternative to paint or wallpaper.

If you live in a home that was built in the last 30 years, chances are your walls are drywall. Although drywall makes a good, flat canvas for many painted finishes, it does not have the smooth touch of a plastered wall.

Plaster has even broadened the scope of another favorite paint technique: stenciling. By applying plaster to the stencil, you can create beautiful embossed patterns, which are stunning when left white or shaded with paint. Plaster has opened up an exciting avenue for borders and textured walls.

Plaster is an age-old medium that is now available in various thicknesses and formulated for easy application to interior walls. You will be familiar with some of the following products; they are easy to find in paint and hardware stores. Ask about any new plaster product lines. Some distributors of Venetian plaster and ornamental gesso are listed in Resources at the back of the book.

ROLLERS

Either split-foam or medium-pile rollers are required to apply paint to a rough plaster surface.

BRUSHES

For painting over stucco, you will need a standard paintbrush to cut into the edges and corners. It is also used to apply Venetian plaster to trimwork.

TROWELS AND SPATULAS

These come in rectangular or spade-shaped, flat pieces of metal with an attached handle. They are used to scoop up and apply the plaster product to the surface. Clean frequently with water and dry. Stainless steel is best because it won't rust.

CAULK, SPACKLE

These plaster-based products, which come already mixed and ready to apply, are used to repair cracks and holes in plaster or drywall. They are formulated with additional hardeners and thickeners and dry quickly. After cleaning out any loose plaster and debris from a damaged area, apply the spackle with a spatula or a putty knife. It will shrink slightly when dry (some products shrink more than others). Apply a second coat if necessary, let dry, then sand flat to the surface. Caulk is absorbent and must be sealed with a primer before being painted.

PLASTER OF PARIS

This plaster product is formulated for molding. The mold dries to a pure white finish that must be primed with shellac before being painted. Instructions for mixing and pouring a mold come with the product.

ORNAMENTAL GESSO

This is thicker than the gesso that artists brush onto their canvases to make a smooth surface for painting. Ornamental gesso has acrylic resins, which make it strong and flexible and help to prevent dripping and drooping when it is being applied to a vertical or overhead surface. It is used to create embossed borders (see gesso border, page 96) and embellish walls, panels, and furniture.

This product comes in clear or white. You may add metallic paste to the clear gesso; you can add universal tint to the white gesso or paint over it when it has dried. It does not require a prime coat. When stenciling with gesso, apply a coat about $\frac{1}{8}$ inch thick over the stencil with a spatula, remove the stencil carefully, and let dry. It takes about 4 hours to dry, depending on the thickness.

VENETIAN PLASTER

Venetian plaster is a type of plaster used for decorative purposes. It has marble dust added to it, unlike traditional stucco. It can be applied as a matte Mediterranean-style wall, or it can be burnished to an elegant high sheen with a trowel or spatula. There are several brands on the market, and it's important to read the individual instructions carefully.

What makes these plasters interesting is that they can be precolored using universal tints. You may tint the plaster yourself or have it done at the paint store. The advantage of pretinting is that scrapes and dents won't show up as white on your finished surface because the color is saturated throughout the plaster layer. The easiest way to apply Venetian plaster is in thin skim coats of one or more colors.

Venetian plaster is semithick and easy to apply with a spatula or a plasterer's trowel. For trimwork, you may use a small brush. The plaster dries in 15 to 30 minutes, depending on how thick a coat you have applied.

The tinted plaster dries 40 percent lighter than the color you see when mixing, so before you start on the walls it's a good idea to do a sample board first to be sure of how the final combinations will look.

TIPS FOR APPLYING PLASTER

1. Work with 2 spatulas, one in each hand. Pick up some of the plaster with 1 spatula. When you are in position at the wall, take a small portion onto the applying spatula and smear it on.

2. Hold the spatula at an angle between 45 and 80 degrees to the surface.

3. Work from only one side of the spatula, applying and then going back over the applied patch. It doesn't matter what direction your strokes run. Cross-hatching is the customary application, which means smearing on and taking off the plaster in small *V*s or *X*s.

4. Do not overload the spatula. You are applying one thin skim coat at a time.

5. Work in strips from the top of the wall down. If you are blending colors (layers) of plaster, work in manageable sections of about 4 square feet.

6. Keep the spatulas clean; a buildup of drying plaster will interfere with a smooth application.

7. When the first layer is dry, sand off any nubbles.

8. After the surface is finished and sanded, wipe it down with a damp cloth to remove the plaster dust. (Plaster at this stage is still porous. Water will soak in, darken the plaster, then dry lighter again.

9. If you wish to seal the plaster, you may apply an acrylic varnish, a glaze coat, or a water-based wax that is sold with the Venetian plaster.

Specialty Wall Coverings

Although I am not a great fan of wallpaper, it has its place when a particular design is desired. I do love some of the specialty wall coverings, and I am thrilled that they are becoming popular once again. There are two embossed wall-covering products, invented more than a hundred years ago in England, that make a superb addition to any collection of decorating solutions. They are Anaglypta and Lincrusta, and I believe they are holding up at least half the walls in Britain. These products, which are thick enough and strong enough to cover up the cracks and bumps in aging plaster, are meant to be painted. When you are tired of the color and want to redecorate, you repaint rather than remove the wall covering.

Both of these products come in a series of original designs that add historic character to any room. They make an exciting background for painted finishes such as verdigris or simply a rubbed glaze to highlight the beautiful patterns.

ANAGLYPTA

Anaglypta, a strong embossed paper made from cotton fibers, is manufactured in England in the same factory that produced it 100 years ago. The paper and design are made and rolled out at the same time, in some cases using the original rollers. The paper comes in rolls of 20½ inches by 33 feet for covering walls and ceilings. It comes in perforated rolls for creating dados, as I have done on page 90, and borders and friezes as well. It is available wherever wallpaper is sold.

HOW TO APPLY ANAGLYPTA AS A DADO OR BORDER

1. The pattern is printed in 36″ increments. Unroll the Anaglypta and cut the paper along the perforations.

2. Apply heavy-duty vinyl adhesive to the back of the paper with a brush. Be sure to cover the entire surface, including all the embossed valleys and indentations.

3. Wait 10 minutes for the paper to absorb the glue. The paper will stretch out a bit as it absorbs the moisture.

4. Place the paper in position on the wall. Use a level to keep it straight. Don't worry if there are small gaps between the paper and parts of the trim. These can be filled with spackle before you paint.

5. Press the paper to the wall with your fingertips, then a brush. Do not use a roller; it will depress the embossed design. As the paper dries, the relief work will return to its original height. Let dry completely.

6. Prime with water-based primer. Adding a little color to the primer helps you see any areas you've missed. Use a brush to get into all the indentations. Let dry. The Anaglypta is now ready for plain paint or a painted finish.

LINCRUSTA

Lincrusta was invented by the son of the man who invented linoleum; he wanted to simulate the same durable, hard-wearing qualities of linoleum in a wall covering. You can actually smell the linseed oil in the Lincrusta. It is very thick and comes embellished with high-relief patterns in a series of original designs, such as the Adam frieze on page 103. It is too heavy for application on ceilings, but it makes an exceedingly durable covering for high-traffic areas such as hallways and kitchens and commercial sites such as bar fronts and restaurant dados.

Although Lincrusta is more expensive than any paper border, it costs far less than new plaster moldings. Once it is applied, you need only repaint to change the mood of your room. A little Lincrusta makes a big statement as a stunning border or centered on a chimney

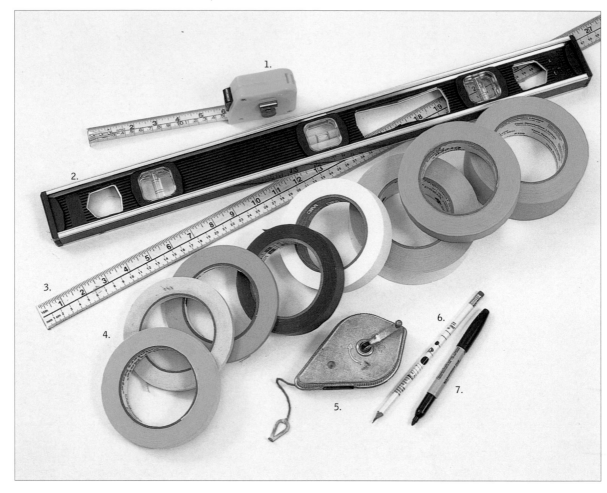

breast. Lincrusta comes in 21-inch-by-33-foot rolls for wall covering. Dado panels are cut and packed flat, and friezes and borders are available in rolls that are 10 inches to 19 inches high and 33 feet long. Lincrusta is paper backed; the relief work doesn't penetrate all the way through the product, as it does with Anaglypta.

HOW TO APPLY A LINCRUSTA BORDER

1. Cut the Lincrusta into manageable sections; it is heavy.
2. Soak the strips in a bathtub for half an hour to make them flexible and pliable enough to handle. Lincrusta is impregnable to water.
3. Apply heavy-duty vinyl adhesive to the back with a brush. Cover the entire surface.
4. Position the Lincrusta on the wall; press it with your hands, then a brush. Any gaps at the ceiling or moldings may be filled with caulk and painted out.
5. Prime with an oil-based primer, then let dry. The Lincrusta is now ready for paint.

Measuring

If you have decided to apply your painted finish in a pattern such as squares, diamonds, or stripes you will need to mark out the design over the entire surface so that the pattern is even. In the case of squares or diamonds, if you begin the pattern at the edge of the wall or floor, the chances are the completed design will look awkward, and your room will be off balance. By marking off from the center, any incomplete pattern repeats will occur equally, and at the edges. Or, if you prefer to end with a complete pattern, simply mask off the excess and make it a border (see Cottage Floor, page 119). The following guidelines pertain to wall, floor, and ceiling surfaces.

MEASURING TOOLS

You will need a pencil, an eraser, a straightedge ruler, a right angle ruler, a level, chalk line, low-tack masking tape, and, if making a template, foam core or cardboard and a sharp knife.

A **chalk line** is a long string that pulls out of a chalk-filled container. It is an indispensable tool for marking out quick and accurate lines. These are easily removed. The free end of the string is tied to a metal ring that acts as a weight and can be used as a plumb line to give you a true perpendicular line when working on a wall (or any vertical surface). Also, if you are working by yourself, the ring can be hooked in position over a nail while you walk the line to the other end of the surface and press it into position. To make a mark, hold the string taut to the surface with one hand and with the other hand, pull the string back a few inches, then let go. The resulting "ping" of the chalky string against the surface will leave behind a straight chalk line. If you do not have a chalk line, stretch out a string from alternate corners, tape down every 2 or 3 feet to secure, and draw several points along the string with a pencil. Remove the string and join the dots with a ruler.

A **level** is a metal or plastic straightedge with one or two small containers of liquid set into it. The level of the liquid will tell you when your line is straight—either horizontally or vertically.

A **right angle ruler** is used to check that your grid lines are perfectly square. Once you have found the surface center and two midpoint lines, you can use this ruler to draw your grid.

MAPPING OUT A GRID

With a chalk line, find the center of the surface by running diagonal lines from corner to corner, creating a cross. They will intersect at the center. Next find the midpoint of the surface edges and join them, intersecting the center point.

For a grid of **squares**, measure and mark the size you want from the midlines and center point out, and join points using the chalk line or right angle ruler.

For a **diamond** pattern, continue to lay down diagonal lines parallel to the original corner-to-corner diagonals. Keep the spaces between the opposing lines the same.

Another method for creating diamonds is to cut out a **template** from a piece of foam core or cardboard. With a marking pen, draw registration lines on the template connecting opposing corners. Mark off a grid on the surface of the wall or floor as described above to match up with your template. Position the template over the surface's center point, and use the level held along a registration line to ensure it's straight. Trace the diamond shape onto the surface with a pencil. Remove the template, and, using your grid lines or ruler to keep the overall design balanced, reposition your template and trace again until the design is complete.

MASKING OFF THE PATTERN

Once you have the pattern mapped out on the surface, tape around each pattern to be filled in. Position the tape just over the chalk or pencil lines so they can be removed when you are finished. If you paint over a pencil mark with a glaze, it will be visible when you are done.

If you want a grout line or border around each square or diamond, center the tape over the pencil or chalk line. The width of the tape will be the size of the grout space and the base coat the color of the grout.

If the colors in the design are butting up against each other, mask off one color, fill it in, remove the tape, and let it dry completely. Then mask off the second color.

For clean corners or points on squares and diamonds, cross the pieces of tape neatly over each other and press down firmly so the paint will not leak.

Always use low-tack masking tape, and remove it immediately. Don't wait for the paint or colored glaze to dry so that you can easily wipe off any leakage.

AVOID MISTAKES

When painting alternate colors or patterns, mark the spaces **not** to be painted with a taped or penciled *X*. Stand back and check your plan before painting.

PHOTO FINISH

An important key to a professional finish is that you are never aware what tools were used to create the look. Take time to erase the evidence. Remove all grid lines either as you complete a section or at the end. Chalk lines are easily wiped away with a damp cloth. Use an eraser for pencil lines.

Yellow

Yellow is the brilliance of sunshine, the tang of fresh lemon, the soft, earthy hues of ocher, or the glitter of gold. It's a happy color, and except in its palest shades, full of spirit. A delicate pale yellow is perfect for a nursery; it's calm and peaceful, just the right mood for a quiet space. The brighter, bolder hues throw off energy and are well suited for a kitchen or a playroom. Yellow also is a country color, reminiscent of farmhouse kitchens when coupled with Provençal blue and/or a crisp white. Deeper, more mellow shades of yellow range from earthy ochers to the rich luster of gold. These colors are full of atmosphere and are perfect for creating warmth and sophistication in a study or dining room. There are probably more shades of yellow than any other color, but it's easy to make a mistake with yellow when picking a shade from paint chips. Remember that paint always dries darker when it's on your walls, so

go one shade lighter. If you discover that the color is far too vibrant once it's on the wall, a simple solution is to reduce any paint left over with white paint and rag or colorwash this lighter shade over the first color.

- Sunshine—A happy color, sunshine is great with white trim and blue accessories.
- Metallic—There are many shades of gold ranging from yellow to red. Luxurious when used on trim-work and furniture, lamps and other accessories, metallics can also be applied as a dramatic finish to walls and ceilings.
- Ocher—Earthy Mediterranean yellows are ideal mixed with glaze to create aged surfaces. Ocher is a fabulous background for any room, old or modern.
- Primrose—This soft yellow is often used for children's rooms and sunny kitchens. Primrose is a good base color for richer ocher glazes.

Blue

There is a shade of blue to match any mood or purpose, from the ubiquitous blues of the sky and the sea to the dark, regal tones of sapphire. Blue can be sophisticated or sporty, hot or cool, or fresh or subdued, depending on what colors it is mixed with. Old, or vintage, blues originally came from the land, either from berries or the far more expensive lapis lazuli, a natural gemstone. Scandinavian blue is a cool blue with a small amount of gray added to it. This is a peaceful color, stunning with white trim in a bedroom. Mid-tone blues, such as cornflower, are some of my favorites. They have a touch of red in them—not quite enough to make them violet, but the right amount to give a hint of warmth. The exotic jewel tones are best used in a dramatic dining room setting.

- Historic—Originally produced from the dye of berries, historic blues are perfect for country homes, for antiquing furniture, or in a masculine-style room. Trim should be off-white, cream, or taupe.

- Scandinavian—Scandinavian blues are soft and subtle. The slight touch of gray in these colors imbue them with warm sophistication. These blues can be used well in both country and city homes.

- Cobalt—Sophisticated on walls ragged or frottaged over a paler blue, cobalt is fabulous with gold or silver accessories. It is used mostly in rooms reserved for entertaining.

- Cornflower—A touch of red is added to create this fresh blue, which is a favorite for bedrooms and children's rooms. Cornflower is stunning with yellow accents and fresh white trim.

RIGHT: *A soft Wedgwood blue in this dining room is a cool complement to the luxurious furnishings.*

LEFT: *Trompe l'oeil sheers were painted in a luminous sea-foam green directly onto the walls of this romantic bedroom.*

Green

In decorating, we often think of green as a safe color; it's the color of grass and leaves, Mother Nature's own backdrop—how can we go wrong? There is an enormous array of greens available. The muted characteristics of vintage and mossy greens look good rubbed into wood paneling, perfect for a den or a period dining room. The deep tones of emerald green and forest green are more sophisticated and look beautiful paired with antique wood furniture and Oriental carpets. Vibrant apple greens and chartreuse complement contemporary homes, but they are also cheerful in a child's room. Paler greens such as pistachio work wonderfully with natural accessories such as sisal carpets, wicker furnishings, cottons, and linens.

- Heritage—These historic colors are tinted with a touch of gray to give a vintage look and are most often used for country-style living.

- Chartreuse—Recently very popular again, chartreuse is ideal for walls in contemporary homes. A lively green that goes well with colorful accessories.

- Pistachio—This young color looks best when mixed with glazing liquid and applied as a paint finish. Pistachio can be used in most rooms and works well with both antique and modern furnishings.

- Hunter—One of the more traditional colors, hunter is often used in dining rooms. Rich and elegant with cream trim and gold accessories, it also complements chintz and country furnishings.

Red

Red cannot be ignored. Its bold strength of character demands your attention, and it is understandable why such a scene-stealer might not be your first choice as a decorating tool. But the heat and passion of such a fiery color can be used to great effect throughout the home. Antique or historic red, what you think of as barn red, is well suited as an accent color for trim-work, furniture, and doors. By adding a little blue to red, you get the crimson and wine shades that are richer and more luxurious, perfect for an elegant dining room. Candlelight glowing around a red room can be mesmerizing. But because red is such an active and arousing color, it's also a bit tiring, so don't paint rooms that are in constant use fire-engine red. Earthy reds are muddier, and easier to live with, as they have an old look that generates an atmosphere of warmth. If red walls scare you, add touches to enliven a space—

maybe a red rug, or lampshade, or just a vivid vase of red roses.

- Chinese—This vibrant, bright red can be used with either fresh white trim or off-white and cream for a more subdued style. Black accessories and trim create a classic Oriental flair.

- Country—The traditional barn red color was originally produced by mixing the pigments from blood and berries. This antique red is ideal in country homes, especially on trim, doors, and cabinetry.

- Burgundy—This opulent red is often seen in dining rooms. It is quite drab in a flat finish, but stunning in a semi- or high-gloss sheen, accessorized with plush velvets and tapestry fabrics.

- Pimento Red—A Mediterranean, orangy red, probably best suited to small areas or rooms for entertaining.

Terra-cotta

The color of clay and bricks, and the multiple shades of terra-cotta tiles, these earth tones are warm, inviting, and easy to live with. It is the color I always use when I want to re-create the look of aged Mediterranean sun-bleached walls. Generally, terra-cottas cover quite a wide range of shades from pale pink to dark orange and deep earth reds. Try rubbing all three shades over a surface and watch how the light plays with these wonderful colors. Terra-cotta in its pure form can be very heavy and opaque, but by rubbing it on over a light base coat, you break up and soften the color beautifully. Because terra-cottas enhance any style and combine effortlessly with most colors, they are one of the most fashionable and enduring of all decorating colors. They are ideal for Mexican, Santa Fe, or Mediterranean rooms.

These four shades of terra-cotta span the clay colors found in Spanish tiles, Mexican pots, and old, sun-bleached Mediterranean walls. Terra-cotta colors work much better as a rubbed or antique finish rather than an opaque covering, where they can appear rather heavy.

- Terra-cotta with an ocher tint
- Terra-cotta with a brown tint
- Terra-cotta with an orange tint
- Terra-cotta with a red tint

LEFT: *The look of huge terra-cotta tiles was painted over cement balcony walls using a mixture of terra-cotta colors. The decorative scheme blends harmoniously with these warm shades to create a sunny outdoor room.*

White

White is clean, fresh, and synonymous with a feeling of space and light. It is considered a safe decorating color in that no one will find it offensive. However, a white surface can create many problems because white hides nothing. Cracks, dirty fingerprints, food, and heating deposits all stand out and even seem magnified against a white background. A textured painted finish produced with layers of creamy whites or dove grays makes a lush and dramatic backdrop for artwork. White walls complement natural wood trim and furnishings, especially mixed with richly textured fabrics and soft stenciled borders. In an all-white room the eye will be drawn to shapes and patterns. There are hundreds of shades of white, from refrigerator white, which has a bluish tone—the least recommended because of its coldness—to off-white and antique whites which are softer and provide the best base coat for most pale painted finishes. Take any color you love—a delicate apple green, a primrose yellow, a cornflower blue—add a few drops to a gallon of white paint, and you will have a gorgeous off-white.

- Off-white—This soft white is ideal for trim and woodwork.
- Antique White—A slightly creamy white that works well with country colors, it is a good base for many painted finishes.
- Tinted White—A few drops of pale pink were added to a gallon of white to produce this pastel white.
- Gray White—This contemporary white is ideal for modern living. It is a good white to incorporate into faux stone finishes.

RIGHT: *This all-white bathroom demonstrates the many different shades and sheens of white from the flat creamy white on the walls to the semigloss off-white on the woodwork to the high gloss of the white marble backsplash.*

Neutral Colors

Neutral colors are derived from the earth: pale woody tones of cream and beige, the soft yellow of sisal or rush matting, stony grays and taupes, and withered browns of dried flowers. They make an impressive natural palette that is the easiest color group to work with. These peaceful, soothing shades work wonderfully alongside each other, or with other earth tones such as muddy greens and reds. But they can also look spectacular brightened and accentuated by a white trim or a dash of vivid color running through your upholstery fabric, throw pillows, or carpet.

Neutral colors are often chosen because they are safe, but they can also be combined to create marvelous texture and depth. My favorite use for these colors is in a stone blocking painted finish where limestone, sandstone, and heavy gray stone are all produced by mixing these natural hues.

- Wheat—The color of sisal matting and grass-cloth walls.
- Taupe—A popular neutral background for walls. Works well in country and contemporary settings.
- Mushroom—A classic color to complement off-white borders and trim; contemporary with the new modern browns.
- Stone Gray—Ideal for monochromatic rooms with highlights of red or blue.

RIGHT: *Bold stripes
in café au lait
brown and an
ornate metallic
border create a dis-
tinctive entrance.
See page 103.*

Brown

Although "brown" may sound drab, it takes on a whole new resonance when you conjure up images of hot and frothy coffee colors like cappuccino, caffè latte, and mocha. This warm color group is back in fashion and can look as traditional or modern as you choose; it's all in the mix. For a more minimal or modern approach, contrast coffee browns with hot tropical color accents in turquoise, hot pink, or lime green. By adding a gloss coat to your painted surface, you can create a sleek, mirrorlike finish that looks right at home with hard-edged or sculpted furniture, metal, and glass. Brown is most commonly used on floors as a stain, in colors ranging from piney yellow to mahogany and cherry to brown oak. Or use the same colors in paint to replicate the look of wood, called *faux bois*. Over the last couple of years metallic paints have become very popular, and therefore more available. A simple way of adding lavish touches to any room is to apply some bronze or copper paint to architectural details or even on a ceiling.

- Chestnut—When this deep brown is mixed with glaze and applied over a lighter base coat it becomes an authentic color for many faux wood finishes.
- Bronze—A metallic color usually applied as an elegant accent, but can also be stunning on walls or a ceiling.
- Coffee—Coffee colors are used to punch up neutrals, creams, or off-whites. Soft and soothing, they are a popular shade for the living room or bedroom.
- Brick Brown—A reddish brown ideal for country homes. Complements greens, blues, and reds. Often used on exteriors.

Black

Black has a long-standing place in interior decorating, where it's most commonly used as an accent to offset other colors. Architects love the minimalist qualities of black and white that allow the building materials and lines of the room to take center stage. Black can be modern, where it's often used with a high gloss, but it can also be more rustic when low-sheen black paint is rubbed and faded. Black teams up with white in many classic partnerships, of which the black and white diamond is the most familiar, and one of my favorite floor treatments. Smaller checkerboard patterns are found everywhere from country folk motifs to the stenciled blocks of the modernistic designer Charles Rennie Mackintosh. Black and white stripes are tailored classics, while a colored contrast stripe against black is more contemporary. A touch of black will always add punch to any decorating scheme.

- Solid Black—A true black is stunning when the finish is high gloss. Superb on floors, panels, trim, or furniture.

- Slate—Gray black can be sophisticated when used in elegant dining rooms, or rustic in country homes. This matte black takes its cue from the surrounding style.

- Aubergine—By adding a touch of red and blue to black, this exotic color is produced. Magnificent on dining room walls lit by candlelight.

- Blue Black—The addition of blue pigments to black paint produces this navy. Traditional for nautical themes or perfectly complemented by gold or silver.

LEFT: *One of my favorite uses of black is in a traditional black-and-white diamond floor.*

decorating with paint and plaster

Much of what we do when we decorate is done to change a room's perspective. In doing so, we adapt all the permanent and transitory elements of a room to suit the way we live. We paint walls, hang curtains and pictures, and set up beds, tables, chairs, and lamps in a manner that makes us feel comfortable and at home. Walls, floors, and ceilings are the permanent features of every room, and therefore the backbone of any decorating scheme. Though these elements cannot be moved easily, with a little work and imagination their strengths can be played up and any weaknesses minimized.

OPPOSITE: *I added sumptuous details, such as a faux leather wall finish and a touch of metallic paint, to a Victorian room with beautiful moldings. See pages 63 and 126 for complete instructions.*

walls

In homes featured on the pages of upscale architecture and decorating magazines, wall surfaces are often white or a pale, neutral color. The main attractions in these rooms are the fabulous and expensive works of art hanging on the walls, and the antique or designer sofas and tables. But we all don't have priceless furniture and accessories to feather our nests, and the good news is they aren't necessary to have a stylish home. For most of us, the challenge is how to create a mood in our home that will be uplifting, satisfying, and affordable. With that in mind, the walls are the best place to start.

The shape, size, and condition of your walls are important factors in your choice of finishes. Whether the walls are drywall or plaster, bumpy or cracked, the versatility of paint and plaster makes anything possible, from simply camouflaging faults to creating a rich, lush ambience in a plain, boxy room. Walls act as a backdrop, a blank canvas ready to accept whatever design you choose. Remember, however, that whereas a painted finish is easily changed later on with a new base coat or possibly a coat of primer, a textured plastered finish is permanent unless it is sanded down.

THE MAGIC OF COLOR

Everyone recognizes the phenomenal impact of color. It is the most powerful tool we have for creating atmosphere or mood. The power of color is heightened or diminished by the way we apply it—as an opaque covering, a painted finish, or a tinted plaster. An opulent effect such as faux leather is more luxurious than just a coat of paint. A simple technique such as colorwashing enables you to apply varying tones of one color onto a wall without the heaviness of solid color, or it can be used to soften a wall color that has proved to be too vivid.

WALLS IN POOR REPAIR

Old walls have cracks, nail holes, and peeling paint or wallpaper, and they are probably dirty. You will have to do some repair work and cleanup before you can apply any new finish or it won't last. (See preparation, page 14.) Some walls will never be perfectly smooth unless new drywall is installed. However, the marvelous thing about a painted finish is that the added texture and dimension you've created with a tinted glaze and a brush, rag, or sponge hides a myriad of sins. An irregular surface may even intensify the beauty of a distressed or frescoed wall.

GIVE NEW WALLS CHARACTER

In older homes it's the bumps, scrapes, cracks, and nail holes that give the rooms character. In modern homes, smooth, new drywall is clean and functional but often boring. But these unblemished surfaces do give us a fine canvas to work on. A painted finish will provide the illusion of texture and depth that's missing, and any painted or tinted plaster finish will be sumptuous to the touch as well as to the eye.

PLAY WITH PATTERN

Stencils and stamps, all kinds of brushes, and even simple household tools can be used to create any motif you can imagine, from traditional ivies and florals to classic

OPPOSITE: *Bold pattern and color update walls in an old apartment dining room. This fabulous finish was accomplished with a simple colorwashing technique. Then over the semi-dry paint, water was finely dripped from ceiling to floor, producing pale streaks down the walls. For instructions on how to measure and mark off the diamonds, see page 32. For colorwashing techniques, see page 53.*

stripes, diamonds, and panels. Patterns are easy to apply to a wall with paint or plaster.

By creating your own design, you're able to play with the size and placement of the motifs, customizing them to fit your space. Pattern is an ideal solution for odd or uneven walls and surfaces. Look at the bathroom walls I spruced up with freehand curlicues on page 161.

A pattern applied with plain paint can be a little harsh. Your new wall finish will be far more appealing if the pattern, as well as the background, is textured or at least softly blended.

TACTILE PLASTERED FINISHES

Plastered wall finishes are created using either tinted plaster or plain white plaster over which paint is applied. The good thing about a tinted plaster finish is that it makes the walls impervious to chips and scratches.

If you live in a new building, the walls are most likely drywall, which provides a lovely flat canvas on which to work. You'll have no trouble applying any painted finish you like. But if you want to give these new walls an aged or weathered appearance, why not go a step further by adding a thin coat of tinted plaster, which will make the walls seem more authentic.

Of course, fresh plaster is also perfect for walls that have aged on their own; just use it creatively to patch areas that need attention. People who gain the confidence to work with plaster often find it an easier medium to work with than paint.

TIPS FOR: *how to paint a professional finish on a wall*

1. Water-based glazing liquid extends the short drying time of latex paint, but only by 10 to 30 minutes, depending on the manufacturer; different brands vary greatly. When applying a painted finish to a large surface like a wall you must work quickly, so it's easiest to use a partner.

2. Work on one wall at a time, and don't leave to answer the phone or make a cup of tea until it is complete. Before you begin, mask off the edges of the adjoining walls, as well as trimwork, with low-tack tape. When one wall is finished and thoroughly dry, usually 2 to 4 hours, move on to the next. Mask off the edges of the finished wall to protect it and continue. This way you'll have perfect corners with no mistakes.

3. Start at the top of the wall and work down, in 3- or 4-foot sections. One person can apply the glaze with a brush or roller, while the other manipulates the glaze as required. To achieve a consistent result, it's best for each person to stick to one job for the duration, as everyone has his or her own touch and even the same pattern can look different when done by different people.

4. When working in sections, apply the next section of glaze quickly overlapping the still-wet first section by about 1 inch. This is called keeping a wet edge. If the glaze has dried before you overlap, you will wind up with a seam line in your finished pattern. It is very difficult to correct this once the wall starts to dry, but if it happens and if the seam bothers you, wet the wall, wipe off the glaze, and start again.

5. A perfect painted finish never shows the tools used to create it. Be careful to eliminate any harsh brush strokes and roller marks with a soft rag or softening brush as noted in the instructions.

colorwashed walls

Colorwashing is one of the most popular painted finishes because it works with most colors and hides a multitude of sins. A coat of thinned-down paint is brushed or wiped over a white or colored background. The texture you create depends on the tools you use. A rag dipped into the paint, then rubbed over the surface in several tones of a color will give a washed-out, distressed effect rather like old faded Mediterranean walls. A brush crisscrossed over the surface offers a more open-textured, naive appearance.

Colorwashing suits most wall surfaces. When this painted finish is applied to older, cracked or bumpy walls, it actually enhances the surface. New drywall is enlivened and given a much softer appearance than if it was painted with a uniform coat of paint.

Here, I used two tones of terra-cotta glaze and rubbed each one over the surface, as if I was washing the wall with a rag. Instead of using commercial paint, I mixed artists' acrylics with glaze to get truer earth tones, but any water-based paints can be used. You will need very little paint for a whole room, so not only is colorwashing a striking finish, it's also economical.

INSTRUCTIONS

Prepare your surface following the instructions on page 14.

STEP 1: Apply 2 coats of the base coat and let dry for 4 hours.

STEP 2: Prepare the glazes. Work in an area about 3' × 3'. Dip the end of a damp rag into the paler glaze, then rub it over the wall in random patches, just like washing a wall. Leave some spots bare.

STEP 3: Fill in some of the bare spots by rubbing on the darker glaze.

STEP 4: Blend the 2 colors together with a clean rag folded flat. Complete the whole wall in this fashion, taking care to blend the edges of a completed section into the next section before the glaze dries to avoid dark lines.

RECIPE

Using latex paint
1 part paint
1 part water-based glazing liquid

Using artists' acrylics
approximately 2 teaspoons
artists' acrylic paint
4 cups water-based glazing liquid

PAINT AND TOOLS

Base coat
cream latex paint, flat or satin
roller, brush, paint tray

Painted finish
raw sienna and burnt sienna latex
paint or artists' acrylic paint
water-based glazing liquid
mixing containers
clean, soft rags

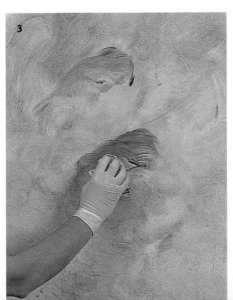

RECIPE

For each colored glaze
1 part latex paint
1 part water-based glazing liquid

PAINT AND TOOLS

Base coat
medium yellow latex paint, satin
roller, brush, paint tray

Painted finish
blood orange–red, pale yellow,
and mint green latex paint, satin
water-based glazing liquid
mixing containers
3″ paintbrushes
newspaper or magazine pages
bottle cork

graffiti

Everything old is said to eventually come back into fashion. That's certainly true of the 1970s look, not only in clothing but also in decorating. Orange and green carpet, Lava lamps, and beanbag chairs are back in style. When I was asked to paint and decorate this teenage girl's basement bedroom, I saw it as a tough challenge. The ceiling was very low, and there was a dated green carpet that she actually liked. I decided to use a modern take on 1970s accessories. The result was a huge success with the teenager, and even with her parents.

Over a medium yellow base coat I painted blood orange–red, pale yellow, and mint glazes in random areas, then blended the colors together with a dry brush. While the surface was still wet, I laid newspaper pages over sections of the glaze, left them in place until the paint was just sticky, then removed them. The newsprint was transferred onto the wall. I also marked some letters into the wet paint using a cork. The effect is lively and was lots of fun to create. If these colors are too vibrant for your taste, you can use the same technique with a different combination of colors—perhaps dark colors and metallic paint—to achieve a sophisticated look.

INSTRUCTIONS

Prepare your surface following the instructions on page 14.

STEP 1: Apply 2 coats of the base coat and let dry for 4 hours.

STEP 2: Prepare the glazes. Working in an area 4' × 4' with a 3" brush, apply the red glaze randomly to 60% of the surface in short vertical and horizontal strokes.

STEP 3: Apply the yellow glaze to 30% of the area in the same way.

STEP 4: Apply the green glaze to 10% of the area in the same way.

STEP 5: Using a dry 3" brush, gently blend the glazes together, moving horizontally and vertically across the wall. Wipe the brush on a rag periodically to keep it dry.

STEP 6: Take a sheet of newspaper with an interesting pattern — the heavier the print, the stronger the transfer — and press it into the wet glaze. Leave it in place until the glaze is tacky. While you are waiting, repeat the painting process on the next section.

STEP 7: Before the glaze dries completely, peel off the newspaper carefully, leaving behind the transfer print. Repeat on the next section.

STEP 8: Inscribe words or symbols into the wet glaze with a cork (optional).

stenciled wall paneling

One question I'm frequently asked is what can be done to hide the look of out-of-date wood-veneer paneling. Removing it can be a risky project, because you don't know the condition of the walls underneath. Painting the paneling to camouflage it is only partially successful, because the panel grooves will still be visible. But with a little ingenuity, the grooves can be made a part of the overall design of a fresh new wall finish.

The walls in this dining room were covered with dark veneer paneling. To begin the makeover, I first applied a chair rail (see page 79 for instructions) to break up the monotony of the paneling. I sanded the veneer and primed the walls with high-adhesive primer, then applied a cream base coat and dry-brushed a slightly darker taupe to break up the flatness of the color. The dado and chair rail were painted red, and then a second coat of teal was added. Once dry, I lightly sanded the surface, revealing areas of red paint to make the finish seem aged. For a finishing touch I chose two folk stencils and painted them vertically onto the wall paneling using heritage colors to complete this country style.

weathered wallboards

The horizontal boards on the interior of this country cottage had layers of white paint built up over the years, and the wall surface was uneven with notches and dents. Instead of trying to camouflage these imperfections, I highlighted them by dry brushing sage green and an oak brown paint over the boards. The resulting translucent effect actually complements the condition of the walls.

INSTRUCTIONS

Prepare your surface following the instructions on page 14. Apply 2 coats of the base coat and let dry for 4 hours.

STEP 1: With a very dry brush, brush the diluted brown paint over the base coat, working along the length of the boards. The paint should go into the wood's imperfections, making them more visible. Let dry.

STEP 2: Working on 2 or 3 planks at a time, apply the sage green diluted paint sparingly with a brush.

STEP 3: With a rag, rub off much of the green, leaving just a soft patina behind, particularly in the cracks and imperfections of the wood.

RECIPE

4 parts latex paint
1 part water-based glazing liquid

PAINT AND TOOLS

Base coat
Cream latex paint, satin
3" or 4" paintbrush

Painted finish
brown and sage green
latex paint, satin
water-based glazing liquid
mixing containers
3" paintbrushes
clean, soft rags

Base coat
white primer or flat white base coat
roller, brush, paint tray

Plastered finish
low-tack masking tape
4" and 6" spatulas or plasterer's
trowels plus one to hold the plaster
yellow- and chartreuse-tinted plaster
bucket of water, sponge

tinted venetian plaster

Venetian plaster has been used in restaurants and hotel lobbies for years. It is popular for its durability; because the plaster is tinted before it's applied, chips or cracks don't show. More and more plaster is being used in homes for the same reason.

If you've never used plaster as a decorating tool, it can seem intimidating, but the truth is that many people actually find it easier to use than paint. The plaster is layered onto a wall, so if there's an area that you are not happy with, more plaster can be added. Patching a painted effect is usually more difficult.

There is one golden rule to remember when using Venetian plaster as opposed to paint. Whereas a paint color dries one or two shades darker, tinted Venetian plaster dries about 40 percent lighter. So before you begin, it's important that you test the colors on a piece of foam core or a small area of your wall.

Once you are satisfied with your chosen colors, the application is fun. Here I used pale yellow and bright chartreuse. I first applied splotches of yellow with a spatula over the surface. Then I plastered the second color over the first layer, blending the colors together and leaving some of the yellow to peek through. Some brands of plaster must be applied over an alkyd-based base coat. Check the manufacturer's instructions carefully.

INSTRUCTIONS

Prepare your surface following the instructions on page 14.

STEP 1: Apply the primer or base coat according to manufacturer's instructions and let dry completely.

STEP 2: To get a clean line, tape along the edge of the wall you are not working on as well as the ceiling and baseboards. Work with one spatula in each hand. Use one spatula to hold a portion of the plaster, the other to take a small blob from this portion and spread it onto the surface. Clean the spatulas periodically with water while you are working so the plaster doesn't dry hard onto the blades.

STEP 3: Take up a portion of the yellow-tinted plaster with a 4" spatula. Work in an area about 10' × 10'. With another 4" spatula, lift a small amount of plaster from the first spatula. Using vertical and horizontal strokes, spread it in thin, random smears onto 50% of the surface.

STEP 4: While the first coat is still wet, apply the chartreuse coat of plaster with a 6" spatula, again smearing on thin layers horizontally and vertically. Cover the entire surface with this plaster, but leave some of the yellow plaster peeking through. Make sure all the white base coat is covered.

3

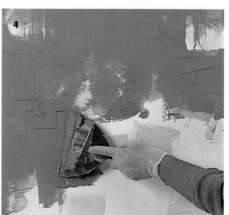

4

NOTE: As the plaster dries, the more you work it with the spatula's edge, the more burnished or shiny it will become. When the colored plaster is completely dry, it will be about 40% lighter in color.

PAINT AND TOOLS

Primer
water-based or oil-based primer,
tinted light brown (check the plaster
manufacturer's instructions)
roller, brush, paint tray

Plastered finish
Venetian plaster, tinted light brown
spatulas
bucket of water, sponge
cheesecloth, enough to cover the walls
fine sandpaper
beeswax (optional)

Glaze
2 parts dark russet latex paint
1 part water-based glazing liquid
mixing container
3" paintbrush

leather walls

The handsome appearance of this study is due to the polished faux leather walls. A leather effect can be produced with paint or plaster, but I think the latter is exceptional. It's a little more complicated to achieve but is well worth the effort.

Here, plaster was skim-coated over the wall. While the thin plaster coat was still moist, lengths of cheesecloth were pressed into it, then a second skim coat was applied. When the cheesecloth was peeled off the still-damp plaster, indentations and markings were produced that gave the appearance of real leather.

Once the plaster had dried and been lightly sanded, a top coat of dark russet glaze was painted over the walls. As an optional finishing touch, beeswax can be rubbed on, then buffed to achieve not only the look but also the feel of real leather.

INSTRUCTIONS

Prepare your surface following the instructions on page 14.

STEP 1: Because your finish is a dark color, you will get better coverage if you tint the primer and the plaster to a paler version of the final color rather than working with stark white. Here, we tinted the primer and plaster light brown. Apply 1 coat of primer and let dry for 4 hours if latex, overnight if alkyd.

STEP 2: Work from the top to the bottom of the wall. With the spatulas, apply a thin, smooth skim coat of the Venetian plaster in a strip (like a wallpaper strip) about an inch wider than the width of the cheesecloth. Clean the spatulas periodically with water.

STEP 3: While the plaster is still wet, take a long strip of cheesecloth and press it onto the plaster strip from top to bottom. When one roll runs out, cut another piece to fit. Don't worry about tears or seams; they will become part of the finish.

STEP 4: Add a second, thinner skim coat of plaster over the cheesecloth so the cheesecloth is sandwiched between the 2 coats of plaster. Start on the next strip, applying skim coat, then cheesecloth, then top skim coat. Repeat until all the walls are covered.

STEP 5: Meanwhile, when a strip of plaster is nearly dry, pull off the cheesecloth. Its imprint will remain in the plaster. The color of the plaster will become lighter as it dries. Let dry completely.

STEP 6: Lightly sand the surface, removing any lumps but leaving the cheesecloth imprint.

STEP 7: Prepare the glaze and brush it onto the plaster. The glaze will give a less heavy look than opaque paint.

Optional: Rub on a coat of beeswax over the dry surface to give the walls the feel and look of leather.

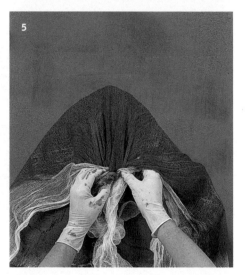

PAINT AND TOOLS

Base coat
candy pink latex paint, any sheen
roller, brush, paint tray

Painted finish
feather duster
white latex paint, same sheen as
the base coat
paper towel

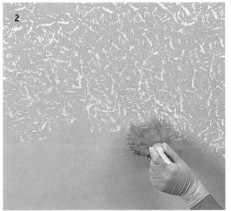

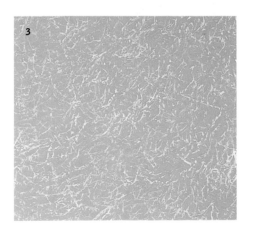

feathering

Many painted finishes are invented by accident or by just playing around with paint. This simple feather technique is a perfect example. I was in the process of painting a client's living room when I picked up a feather duster that had been left on a shelf. I dipped the end into white paint and dabbed it gently over the cream-colored wall. To my delight, a delicate effect of tiny white specks was created. I've used this technique ever since, and no one can guess what tool I use.

In this baby's nursery, a vivid candy pink was given a dreamy appearance by feathering white paint over the surface. If the color you purchased for your walls turns out to be too intense, feathering is an ideal solution to tone it down a notch.

INSTRUCTIONS

Prepare your surface following the instructions on page 14. Apply 2 coats of the base coat and let dry for 4 hours.

STEP 1: Dip the end of a feather duster into white paint and dab off the excess on a paper towel.

STEP 2: Gently dot the feather duster over the surface, starting at the top of the wall and working down.

STEP 3: Keep standing back to review your work to ensure that the pattern left by the duster is fairly uniform.

parchment

I once demonstrated a technique for re-creating the look of antique parchment paper on my television show, and I have never been so inundated with requests for a paint recipe. Perhaps because of its translucent elegance or its simple charm, this is an effect that works well with any type of decor. For this dining room I chose a light ocher glaze over an off-white base coat. Once the glaze was applied, I used a clean rag to gently "crease" the surface.

INSTRUCTIONS

Prepare your surface following the instructions on page 14.

STEP 1: Apply 2 coats of the base coat and let dry for 4 hours.

STEP 2: Prepare the glaze. Work in an area about 3' × 3'. With a brush, apply the glaze in a crisscross motion over the base coat, covering 100% of this area.

STEP 3: To create the creases, with a rag push the glaze to form short, irregular lines.

STEP 4: With the same rag, dab back over areas that have become lightened where you have pushed the glaze into a crease. The lines of the creases should be in a random pattern going in all directions.

NOTE: Instead of latex paint, for a more true yellow ocher either artists' acrylic or powder pigments can be used.

RECIPE

1 part latex paint
1 part water-based glazing liquid

PAINT AND TOOLS

Base coat
off-white latex paint, satin
roller, brush, paint tray

Painted finish
yellow ocher latex paint, satin
water-based glazing liquid
mixing container
3" paintbrush
clean, soft rags

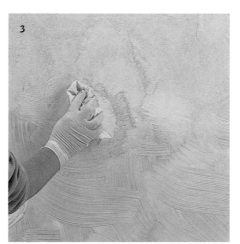

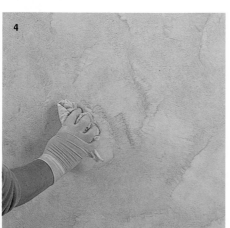

wall panels

One of the most common decorating dilemmas in open-plan homes is how to treat the large expanses of unbroken wall space. There is often no separation between the living room, dining room, and kitchen, or between walls that reach two stories high. I'm often asked if it's possible to have more than one paint color over all, and, if so, where each one should start and stop. Another question I'm asked is if it's feasible to use a decorative painted finish in only one area of a space such as this.

Wall panels have been used for centuries as a solution to decorating problems. They may call to mind an elegant Parisian drawing room or a luxurious mahogany-paneled library, but there is an alternative to real panels. Faux wall panels are an ideal solution to these problems. They trick the eye into seeing different surfaces as opposed to seeing a long, unbroken expanse. The right painted finish will embellish new or old walls.

DEFINE YOUR LIVING SPACE

Plain panels, which are simply sections of color, can be used as a clever decorating trick to divide rooms. If you have one open space for living and dining, paint a single background color, then apply two shades of color in panels to differentiate between the spaces. For example, the panels in the living room area could be pale green and those in the dining area a deeper, more dramatic moss green.

DECORATING THE PANELS

If you don't have wood or plaster panels to decorate, you can make your own with new strips of wood trim or by painting a faux frame around each section (see page 69). Choosing colors for the panels and the walls needs some careful thought, because it's important to keep the contrast between these two colors as close as

RIGHT: *The panels were already in place in this old apartment living room, but the decor seemed tired. To liven it up, I painted the walls cream and rolled a damask pattern onto the panels with a special roller.*

possible. If the panels are framed with wood molding, you can paint the moldings in an accent color or keep them the same color as the wall, depending on the amount of definition you desire. Most finishes work well and are a lot faster and easier to apply within the confines of a panel than over a whole wall. Complex designs, such as marbling, don't suit a large wall.

IN BALANCE WITH OTHER ARCHITECTURAL FEATURES

Wall panels can be used to break up a large wall surface. It could be a very tall wall in a small space with high ceilings, or an unbroken stretch of wall down a long hallway. Panels add interest and balance to these schemes. Paint allows you to imitate any style by producing sections or panels that have the appearance of expensive silk fabric or finely tooled leather.

UNORTHODOX SHAPES AND SHADES

Panels don't have to be rows of matching rectangles on walls, although this is the most common configuration. Instead, irregular patterns can be used to make a wall a focal point. This is a wonderfully fresh way of announcing the start and finish of a designated eating or play area.

LEFT: *This panel is now reminiscent of the flock wallpaper popular in the '40s. See page 22 for more information on specialty rollers.*

TIPS FOR: *planning and preparation for wall panels*

A panel is a square or rectangular section that is set apart from the area around it by a border or a change in color, texture, or height.

To create simple panels:

1. Apply 2 coats of base coat to the entire surface, and let dry completely.

2. Measure the length of your walls, and divide by the number of panels you want plus the space between the panels. There is no set rule for panel size, but the smaller the panels, the more taping you will have to do, and too many panels will make the room too busy. Generally, panels should be positioned 4" to 6" down from the ceiling and 2" to 10" away from baseboards and trim.

3. Mark and mask off the panel sections, using a plumb line, a level, and low-tack tape. This will ensure that the lines are straight, and the corners perfect right angles.

4. Fill in the sections with any painted finish. The base coat will provide the background frame for your panels.

A **frame or border** for each panel can be masked off and painted in. To create the impression that the panels are recessed, paint the frame in light and dark shades according to the room's light source (see page 176). Alternately, the frame can be as simple as a strip of paint, or a freehand design with small geometric patterns, squiggly lines, or flowers and vines. It is not always necessary to add the border decoration to all sides of the panel.

Panels can be added to a plain wall surface by **applying strips of wood molding,** which are available in a variety of styles and sizes at hardware and lumber stores. When you are installing the molding frame, miter the corners for a professional finish. (See instructions for adding a chair rail, page 79.)

If you have built panels with molding, the entire surface of the wall can have the same finish, with the color graduated inside the panels by one or two tones for a subtle contrast.

strié panels

The designer of this elegant dining room had previously applied moldings to the walls to create large panels above the chair rail and smaller ones below it. I painted the area surrounding the moldings a Wedgwood blue, then added a simple painted finish to highlight the inside of these panels. I used a technique called strié, using the same blue paint mixed with a water-based glazing liquid. I pulled a dragging brush through the colored glaze, creating thin textured lines that resemble raw silk fabric. Strié is a sophisticated look that can also be used more casually on trimwork or furniture.

INSTRUCTIONS

Prepare your surface following the instructions on page 14. Apply 2 coats of the base coat and let dry for 4 hours. Protect the area around the panel (the molding or the walls) with masking tape.

STEP 1: Prepare the glaze. With a roller, apply it to the whole panel, being sure to cover 100% of the surface.

STEP 2: While the glaze is still wet, pull a dragging brush vertically through the glaze. You can do this several times until the lines look as straight as possible.

NOTE: When you are applying a strié finish to large walls, work in vertical strips, applying the glaze from top to bottom about twice the width of the roller. Any wider and the glaze will start drying before you can manipulate it to create the finish. If you are working on a large panel where you need a ladder, position it so you can move smoothly from the top of the panel to the bottom.

RECIPE

1 part latex paint
1 part water-based glazing liquid

PAINT AND TOOLS

Base coat
off-white latex paint, satin
roller, brush, paint tray

Painted finish
low-tack masking tape
Wedgwood blue latex paint, satin
water-based glazing liquid
mixing container
roller, brush, paint tray
dragging brush or wide,
hard-bristle paintbrush

faux linen panels

In this studio apartment, simple panels were used to break up a long, plain room. Blocks of faux linen make this space intimate and very young and stylish.

First, I applied a coffee-colored base coat to all the walls. Then I marked and taped rectangles about 4 feet by 6 feet. I painted the panels with a white glaze, then dragged a damp kitchen sponge through the glaze to produce the look of sheer linen. Finally, I traced and painted curlicues down each side of the panels as an extra detail.

RECIPE

1 part latex paint
1 part water-based glazing liquid

PAINT AND TOOLS

Base coat
café au lait latex paint, satin
roller, brush, paint tray

Painted finish
low-tack masking tape
white latex paint, satin
water-based glazing liquid
mixing container
kitchen sponge
pencil
artists' brush
small amount of dark
brown latex paint, satin

INSTRUCTIONS

Prepare your surface following the instructions on page 14. Apply 2 coats of the base coat and let dry for 4 hours. Measure and mask off the panels with tape (following the instructions on page 69). The size and shape of the panels should be in proportion to the size of your room.

STEP 1: Mix the white glaze. Working on one panel at a time, wipe it roughly over 100% of the surface with a damp kitchen sponge using mostly vertical strokes. Rinse and wring out the sponge.

STEP 2: Holding the sponge flat against the surface repeatedly pull it through the glaze from top to bottom, creating the weave of fine linen. The translucent white strokes against the café au lait base do not have to be perfect, but they must move in the same direction. Remove the tape, then wipe off any leaks. Let dry.

STEP 3: Hand-draw a curlicue with a pencil, overlapping the border lines of the panels. With an artists' brush and brown paint mixed with just a bit of glazing liquid, paint over the pencil lines.

pastel metallic panels

Panels do not have to be perfect rectangles on walls. They can be all shapes and sizes, especially when used on a wall that is the focal point of your room. I had fun painting this unusual curved kitchen wall. First, I applied an aluminum base coat to the whole surface; once dry I mapped out a pattern of irregular squares and rectangles. I masked these off with different widths of low-tack tape, then colorwashed each area with a variety of pastel colors. The metallic base coat glowing through the colored glazes produces a luminous effect.

INSTRUCTIONS

Prepare your surface following the instructions on page 14. Apply 2 coats of the base coat and let dry for 4 hours.

STEP 1: Over the dry base coat, mark out a grid of different sizes of squares and rectangles using a ruler and a light pencil line, or a chalk line. Use a spirit level to make sure the lines are straight.

STEP 2: Tape along the lines with ¾" and 1" tape, creating panels and borders of different sizes.

STEP 3: Prepare the glazes. Using a colorwash technique (see page 53), wash the pastel glazes over each shape, one color per panel, being careful not to go over the tape.

STEP 4: Remove the tape carefully. If metallic powders have been used, the walls must be sealed with varnish.

RECIPE

To make pastel glazes
1 part latex paint
1 part water-based glazing liquid

PAINT AND TOOLS

Base coat
aluminum paint, latex
(See metallic paints, page 16.)
roller, brush, paint tray

Painted finish
pencil, eraser, ruler *or* plumb line
and chalk line
spirit level
¾" and 1" low-tack
masking tape
pastel pink, blue, and green latex paint
water-based glazing liquid
mixing containers
clean, soft rags
varnish and brush, if required

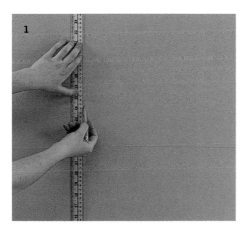

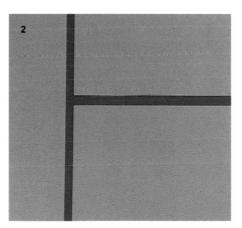

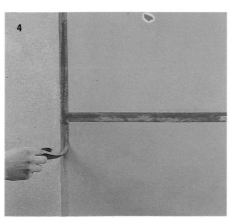

RECIPES

For the latex glazes
1 part latex paint
1 part water-based glazing liquid

For the acrylic glazes
approximately 2 teaspoons
artists' acrylic paint
2 cups water-based glazing liquid

PAINT AND TOOLS

Base coat
white latex paint, flat or primer
roller, brush, paint tray

Painted finish
raw sienna artists' acrylic paint
medium gray, white, dusty pink, and
dark pink latex paint, satin
water-based glazing liquid
mixing containers
white latex paint, flat
3" paintbrushes (optional)
clean, soft rags
1" low-tack masking tape
sanding sponge

frescoed panels

A magnificent hallway is the focal point of a Victorian house. Nearly every room upstairs and down looks into the hallway, so I decided to make it an interesting conversation piece. I kept the colors and decor of the rooms off the hallway fairly neutral so they wouldn't compete with the frescoed walls. Instead of spending a great deal of time replastering the walls, which weren't in perfect condition, I worked with the original bumps and cracks and even painted in some new ones.

Fresco is an ancient technique of wall painting. Examples can be seen in ancient Roman murals and Italian Renaissance art. This method of painting comes from the Italian word *frisc,* which means fresh. Colored pigments were mixed with water and painted directly onto wet lime plaster. Once dry, the painting was part of the wall, and, as such, could last for centuries. This method of painting frescoes, although still used by skilled artists, is extremely difficult and labor intensive. But we can paint our own—maybe not quite so elaborate—with latex paint and water.

First, the frescoed base is applied using muted colors, then areas are sanded off to give the illusion of age. Next, the murals or stencils can be applied. Fresco painting seems complicated, but it's really just basic painting and sanding.

INSTRUCTIONS

Prepare your surface following the instructions on page 14. Apply 1 coat of the base coat and let dry for 4 hours, *or* apply the fresco finish straight over white primer.

STEP 1: Prepare raw sienna, medium gray, and 2 shades of pink glazes. For the first fresco layer, apply the raw sienna and medium gray glazes using the colorwashing technique on page 53. The goal is to create a mottled look.

STEP 2: Apply a small amount of flat white paint over this layer with a brush or a rag. Rub and dab, blending any rag or brush marks. This first layer of muted color will show through the top layer. It will also be the color of the taped panels. Don't worry if the paint looks dull; you're creating an ancient-looking undercoat. Let dry completely.

STEP 3: Over this first layer, apply tape to frame your panels (optional). For the second layer of fresco, apply the 2 pink glazes with a rag, then blend them together. It's important not to see traces of the tools you've used, whether a brush or a rag, so continue to blend the glazes until the surface is softly mottled and textured.

STEP 4: Remove the tape immediately, which will reveal the frame.

STEP 5: Once the surface is dry, lightly sand areas to reveal different layers of paint. Choose areas you aren't happy with—perhaps where the tape removed some of the paint. These are good areas to sand back even as far as the white base coat, to make it look as though the fresco has been worn by time.

NOTE: You can paint simple motifs inside the frescoed panels either freehand or with a stencil, or by tracing naive patterns. When dry, sand over your work to age the paintings.

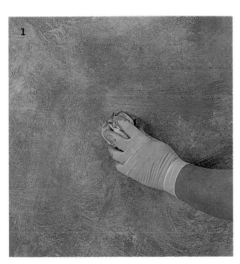

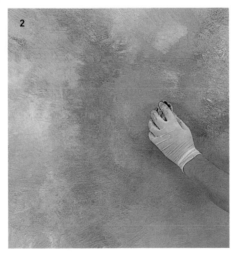

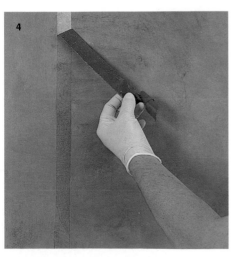

Dados, one of my favorite ways to decorate a wall, are a practical solution to a multitude of decorating problems. When considering what type of paint treatment would suit a particular space, I invariably look at the feasibility of applying a dado around the room. A dado is a band, usually 3 to 4 feet high, on the lower section of a wall. It's topped by a chair rail or an ornamental border.

A dado is an effective way to minimize the impression of height in a room with high ceilings, or offset the impression that you're sitting in a plain box no matter what size your room. If you feel limited by one color or painted finish on the walls, inserting a dado will divide the surface into two distinct sections and offer countless opportunities to mix and blend colors and textures.

Faux finishes can reproduce the look of expensive, luxurious materials such as fine woods, silk, leather, marble, and granite. These finishes would not be suitable or, in some cases, realistic, on whole walls, but applied judiciously to lower walls they can be seen and enjoyed without being overpowering.

DADOS CREATE AUTHENTIC STYLE

Dados were used extensively in Victorian homes. The Victorians did not lounge; they sat upright on solid, wood-back chairs and settees. Hence, the chair rails had a practical as well as a decorative purpose: to protect any wall finishes from the inevitable dents and scratches caused by furniture bumping against them. If your furnishings and taste are Victorian in nature, a dado topped with a chair rail will help you to create an authentic look.

For the same practical reason, chair rails are a signature of almost every country style, but the wall treatments differ. Whereas Victorians used elaborate wallpaper patterns with dark or somber colors, a typical country scheme would include the upper walls simply painted and a dado of stained wood.

REDEFINING A ROOM WITH A DADO

If you live in a home that was built before 1940, chances are your ceilings are anywhere from 10 to 13 feet high. If you don't already have dados in these rooms, you can add one. It will bring the walls down to human scale, creating an area that feels more comfortable and welcoming.

BUILD AESTHETIC AND ARCHITECTURAL INTEREST

In newly built homes, walls are generally about 8 to 9 feet high. Adding a border around the top of the walls pulls the ceiling down even more—not necessarily a good idea. Adding a dado and keeping the upper walls and ceiling light will draw your attention to the lower walls and cause the ceiling to recede.

TIPS FOR:
how to apply a chair rail

If your room doesn't have a dado, you can easily create one. The dividing line between the upper and lower wall generally takes the form of a chair rail, which is a precut molding sold in strips at hardware stores and lumberyards.

The height of the chair rail is optional, but the best rule of thumb is about adult hip height. Never position it in the middle of the wall or it will visually cut the room in half—a disconcerting feeling when the work is done. The rail should run parallel to the floor or baseboard, not the ceiling (walls are seldom even), so measure 3 to 4 feet up from the top of the baseboard and affix the molding with nails.

An alternative to nailing on molding, and one that is far less expensive and much quicker, is to paint a border. Measure as you would for the molded chair rail, then mask off a band approximately 4 inches wide, depending on your design. Always paint the upper walls first, followed by the dado; then remask the chair rail area and fill in with a contrasting color.

OPPOSITE: *For a contemporary room you can't beat the sleek look of metal. Here we have painted a dado to resemble sheet metal—it looks totally authentic, right down to the painted studs.*

brushed steel dado

Believe it or not, you can easily replicate the patina of steel with paint. I find that the effect works best in large panels along a dado, but you could apply it to a whole wall, perhaps in a home office or a hallway. The upper walls in this new condominium were painted a rich café au lait, which along with the steel produces a warm, complementary glow that radiates day and night. To re-create the look of steel, two tones of silver were painted over a black base. Then I painted metal studs around the panels for an industrial touch. First I dipped a pencil eraser in black paint and pressed it on the wall, then I used a touch of white as a highlight.

INSTRUCTIONS

Prepare your surface following the instructions on page 14. Apply 2 coats of the base coat and let dry for 4 hours.

STEP 1: Mask off the panels leaving an ⅛" gap between the panels.

STEP 2: Prepare the glazes. With a brush, apply random strokes of the silver glaze, moving horizontally and vertically on the first panel. Apply to 70% of the surface.

STEP 3: Add patches of the aluminum glaze, filling in some of the gaps and crossing over into some of the silver glaze.

STEP 4: With a clean, dry brush, work in horizontal and vertical strokes to blend the colors, leaving some areas of the black base showing.

STEP 5: With a dry rag, polish the tacky paint, removing more glaze and creating a steel patina.

Always keep your movements linear, moving on the vertical and horizontal. A coat of varnish must be added if you used powdered metallic paint.

RECIPE

1 part latex paint
1 part water-based glazing liquid

PAINT AND TOOLS

Base coat
black latex paint, satin or matte
roller, brush, paint tray

Painted finish
low-tack masking tape
two tones of silver (we used
aluminum and silver latex paint, satin)
water-based glazing liquid
mixing containers
3" paintbrushes
clean, soft rags
varnish (mid sheen) and
brush (optional)

RECIPE

For the colored glazes
1 part latex paint
1 part water-based glazing liquid

PAINT AND TOOLS

Base coat
cream latex paint, satin
roller, brush, paint tray

Painted finish
peach, light gray, viridian green, and
white latex paint
water-based glazing liquid
mixing containers
¼″ low-tack masking tape
fitch or 1″ paintbrush
clean, soft rags
artists' brush or feather (optional)
badger hair or soft-bristle paintbrush
3″ paintbrushes
varnish and brush (optional)

fantasy marble dado

There are about as many paint techniques to reproduce varieties of real marble as there are marble. There's also fantasy marble, which has the look and pattern of actual stone but is reproduced in colors chosen by you, not Mother Nature. The pale yellow, peach, and cream in this bedroom are not reminiscent of real marble colors, but the diagonal movement and shapes produced by the paint are authentic. I've also painted the faux marble into slabs, just like the real thing. The soft shades in the marble are echoed in the whimsical faux sheer fabric that has been painted on the upper wall, and the Greek key border stenciled in bronze adds a magnificent classic touch.

Faux marble works well on floors, fireplaces, furniture, and, of course, walls, but painting an entire wall in faux marble can be overpowering. On a dado, however, this impressive technique looks classic and elegant.

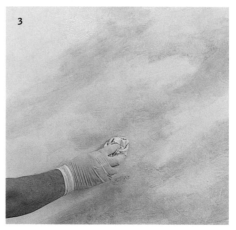

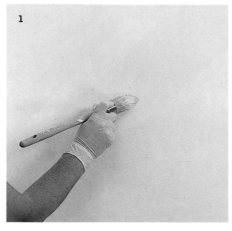

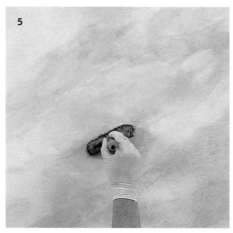

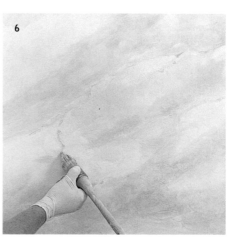

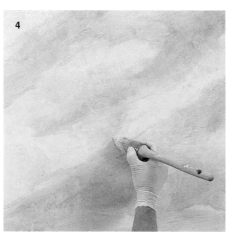

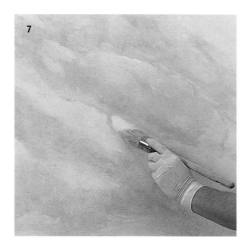

INSTRUCTIONS

Prepare your surface following the instructions on page 14. Apply 2 coats of the base coat and let dry for 4 hours.

STEP 1: Prepare the glazes. Mask off panels about 3' to 4' wide along the dado. Apply the cream glaze over the dry base coat in diagonal drifts, leaving a few gaps. I used a 1" fitch, but any paintbrush will do.

STEP 2: Fill in the gaps with the peach glaze, making sure that 100% of the surface is now covered.

STEP 3: Blend the colors together with a folded rag. Make sure that any brush strokes are softened out.

STEP 4: Using the point of the fitch, a small artists' brush, or a feather, vein the surface with the light gray glaze, following the contours created by the first two colors. Do not wave or curve the veins; real veins are jagged, broken lines.

STEP 5: With the badger brush held at a right angle to the surface, dust the veins lightly to soften and open them up.

STEP 6: Add a few more veins sparingly with the viridian green glaze.

STEP 7: To further highlight the veins and give depth to the marble, fill in areas between veins with a small amount of pure white paint, using the point of the fitch. Play with the glazes until you get the effect of layers of different colors and broken veins. A coat of varnish will give the sheen of real marble.

RECIPE

1 part latex paint
1 part water-based glazing liquid

PAINT AND TOOLS

Base coat
pale blue latex paint, satin
roller, brush, paint tray

Painted finish
1" low-tack masking tape
denim blue latex paint
water-based glazing liquid
mixing container
speckle and dragging tool or
rough wallpaper brush

Optional stencil for stitching lines
Mylar
X-acto knife
marking pen
stencil adhesive spray
stencil brush
small amounts of terra-cotta and dark
blue latex paint

faux denim dado

The faded look of denim is captured with paint in this boy's bedroom. The soft textured effect could work equally well in most rooms using different colors.

I've paneled the dado in patches approximately 3 feet wide, then separated these areas with a thin blue line a little darker than the denim. To add a whimsical (and authentic) touch, I've stenciled a terra-cotta–colored stitch line down the sides of each panel and even put in a half circle to reproduce a pocket. The chair rail (see page 79) is simply a painted strip decorated with metal cowboy boots painted white.

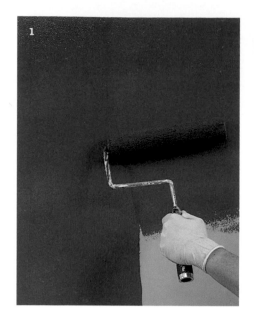

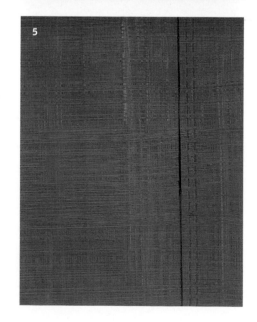

INSTRUCTIONS

Prepare your surface following the instructions on page 14. Use tape to protect the chair rail and baseboards.

STEP 1: Apply 2 coats of the base coat and let dry for 4 hours. Prepare the glaze. Mask off panels or patches in whatever size you want. You'll be working in alternate panels, and the tape will prevent leaks and smudges. Apply the glaze over the base coat, covering 100% of the surface of one panel.

STEP 2: Hold the denim brush firmly against the top of the dado, then pull it vertically through the glaze to create a rough strié effect. Return to the top of the panel and repeat until the whole panel is covered with vertical lines.

STEP 3: Pull the denim brush through the wet glaze horizontally. Work all the way down one panel. This creates the faded weave of real denim. Skip a patch and repeat the process, continuing to work on alternate panels. When dry, return to the beginning and fill in the missing patches.

STEP 4: If you wish, cut out a stencil of stitching lines from Mylar; with a marking pen, draw each line about ½" long. Use stencil adhesive spray to position the stencil. Fill in the stitches using a stencil brush and terra-cotta paint.

STEP 5: As an optional finishing touch, hand-paint a dark blue seam line between the panels.

PAINT AND TOOLS

Base coat
cream latex paint, satin
paintbrush

Painted finish
blue, rust, and sage green
latex paint, satin
foam brush

To make the tools
sponge roller
pencil, ruler
sharp knife
½" masking tape
paint tray
thick cardboard

country tartan dado

I'm always looking for a faster method of creating painted finishes, especially those that involve measuring and taping. I wanted to paint a tartan pattern in this country dining room but wasn't in the mood for lots of work.

With a little ingenuity, I produced a simple pattern that turned out to be bright and cheerful yet rustic—perfect for a country setting. The heritage colors I chose were blue, rust, and sage green. The challenge was to apply all three paint colors over the base coat at the same time. I divided a paint tray into three sections and did the same to a sponge roller. The technique worked brilliantly—all it took was a steady hand. (It's best to practice your design on paper first.)

Above the chair rail I sponged rust-colored paint over the cream base coat. But first I applied leaves (you can use real or plastic) to the wall with low-tack glue. After completing the sponging effect, I removed the leaves and revealed the impressions they left behind.

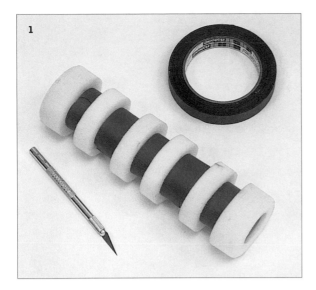

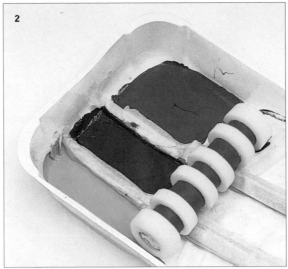

INSTRUCTIONS

Prepare your surface following the instructions on page 14. Apply 2 coats of the base coat and let dry for 4 hours.

STEP 1: To divide the sponge roller into separate sections, measure and draw circles around the sponge with a pencil and ruler. Score the sponge with a sharp knife, making the scoring lines about ¼" deep. You will need 5 cuts to make 6 equal sections. Secure the sponge down at the cut lines by wrapping masking tape tightly around the roller. (Alternatively, you can use sponge rollers that have already been scored; they are used for painting stucco.)

STEP 2: To divide the paint tray into 3 sections (when the roller sits in the tray, 2 roller sections will fit into 1 tray section), with masking tape secure pieces of cardboard in the trough and up and along the ribbed area. The dividers should be no higher than 1". Do not thin the paint with

water or it will leak under the tape. Pour a small amount of the 3 colors into the separate compartments in the paint tray. Carefully roll the sponge roller into the paint, moving back and forth until it is saturated. If parts of the sponge don't get enough paint, add paint to that specific roller section with a paintbrush.

STEP 3: Pull the roller horizontally along the dado, creating 6 naive stripes. Leave a 1" gap and pull the roller through again. Repeat this pattern along the dado. The roller will need more paint after every 2 or 3 times. Stop and readjust your position at every arm's length. After lifting the roller off the surface, be sure to realign it. But remember that you are creating a naive effect; the stripes aren't meant to be perfect. You can fill in any large gaps with a foam brush.

STEP 4: Pull the roller vertically down the dado. Leave a 4" gap between sections. Repeat until you reach the end.

anaglypta dado

Anaglypta, an embossed wallpaper designed to be painted, has always been popular in Britain, where thick wallpapers are commonly used to camouflage bumpy, peeling, and cracked walls and even ceilings. The paper, usually coated with layers of paint, is rarely removed from the wall—because it's often the only thing holding everything together.

Aside from being strong, Anaglypta has decorative purposes, which is why it's becoming more and more popular in North America. It comes in numerous embossed patterns, which can be painted or colorwashed to enhance the design. It's available at decorating stores by the roll for borders, wall coverings, and dados. (See Resources, page 190.)

The dining room in this new home had no ceiling moldings and little trim, so to add some character to this otherwise plain room I added a wooden chair rail. The owners were lovers of the art nouveau period and had several pieces of authentic furniture. To complement these pieces, I applied Anaglypta with a traditional art nouveau design to the dado, which was then rubbed in leaf green to highlight the pattern.

INSTRUCTIONS

Prepare your surface following the instructions on page 14.

STEP 1: Apply the Anaglypta following the instructions on page 30. Using a 3" brush, apply 1 coat of the base coat to 100% of the paper and let dry. This is very important, because the base coat seals the paper.

STEP 2: Prepare the glaze. With a 3" brush, apply the glaze over the Anaglypta, making sure the glaze gets into all the indentations. Work on one panel of paper at a time.

STEP 3: When the glaze dries to tacky, take a smooth folded rag, polish the surface, removing the top layers of the glaze. This highlights the embossed pattern, because the colors are stronger in the indentations.

RECIPE

1 part latex paint
1 part water-based glazing liquid

PAINT AND TOOLS

Base coat
Anaglypta
cream latex paint, satin
3" paintbrush

Painted finish
leaf green latex paint, satin
water-based glazing liquid
mixing container
3" paintbrush
clean, soft rags

borders

OPPOSITE: *A spacious bedroom was given a colonial flavor by stenciling a wide lattice border around the room.*

The prospect of painting and decorating a whole room can be daunting, so it's sometimes helpful to start with a smaller project that will reward you with an immediate face-lift and mood change.

Adding a simple border design to plain walls is an instant and inexpensive way to dress them up. It could also be a way to tie in your walls with other elements in the room, such as lamps, fabrics, and odd pieces of furniture. Trace or copy a motif or shape that you love from the pillow or curtain fabric, or even the scrollwork on a table or chair leg. Alternatively, pick up one or two of your favorite colors.

Awkward rooms are always a challenge. Sloped ceilings, extensions for windows, and inconveniently placed ductwork all pose decorating dilemmas that can often be solved effectively by adding a border. With a border, you get maximum impact in a relatively small space.

CONSIDER YOUR ROOM'S ARCHITECTURE

When choosing a border detail to decorate a room, you will first want to take into consideration the shape of the room, any existing moldings and doors, odd corners or alcoves, and the height and slant of the ceiling. The color and pattern of your border should enhance these features as well as unify the style of the room.

Older homes usually have deep border moldings made from wood or plaster. In spacious rooms with high ceilings, these moldings were often beautifully handcrafted works of art; their ample size, complexity, and visual weight brought the rooms into human scale. If the walls in your home are high enough, the existing molding can be enhanced further by adding a stenciled border directly under it, as I did in my living room, using plaster instead of paint (see page 96).

The newer your house or apartment, the fewer moldings and architectural details it probably has. Although builders continued to install trimwork through the 1950s, in most cases the moldings were smaller and less ornate. Molding is still a worthy detail, however. I usually paint it white to give a fresh frame to whatever wall finish I've chosen.

Homes built in the 1960s and 1970s have little or no molding. Baseboards and window and door trim are most likely no more than 3-inch strips of wood or plastic and are not meant to be highlighted. I prefer to make them disappear by painting them the same color as the walls, then adding a border that will either create or bring out something of interest in the room, such as a handsome doorway or set of windows.

Most modern homes and apartments have no interior details unless they have been specifically requested. Rooms typically have boxed-off ductwork and plumbing jutting down from the ceiling or in awkward spots such as at the center of a long wall. To add character and interest to such a plain, unappealing backdrop, I would run a border pattern around the room at ceiling or chair rail height and wrap it around anything in its path, like the ductwork boxes, or even across woodwork and window treatments.

TIPS FOR: *applying a border*

1. A border should be at least 4″ deep and must be straight. Use a plumb line and level and mark and measure down from the ceiling.

2. Take into consideration other architectural details in the room, such as ducts and window and door frames.

3. When you are working with a repeated pattern, start in the least conspicuous place in the room, like behind a door, so it won't matter if the repeated pattern does not join up perfectly.

4. If your ceilings are low, a border can pull them down even more, producing a boxy effect. In this case, keep the design light or run a border around doorways and windows or even as a chair rail.

5. Keep the color and scale of the border in proportion to the room.

6. Because a border covers a small, restricted area, it's a good place to experiment with an elaborate painted finish.

PLATE RAILS

Plate rails, a popular decorating feature in the 1930s and 1940s, are 2- to 4-inch-deep lengths of trim that run around the room about 18 inches down from the ceiling. If you have one of these, and you don't collect plates, it is an ideal panel for a decorative finish. Stencils, stamps, or blocks can be used successfully to embellish this space, and with a little imagination this area can become a new focal point of the room. I had fun stenciling the profiles of family members on a plate rail in a classic-style den (see page 107).

If you don't have a plate rail but the idea appeals to you, simply mask off and paint a wide band, or install molding as you would for a chair rail (see page 79).

STENCILED BORDERS

One of the most traditional ways of creating a border is with a stencil, and there are literally hundreds of designs and motifs available. All border stencils come with one of two methods for repeating the pattern. There may be an image at each end of the cutout pattern that is drawn to fit over your last cutout; this will keep the space between repeats perfectly even. Or, your stencil may have registration marks—tiny holes that mark the top, bottom, and sides of the stencil. You apply paint to these holes as you work, and they act as a guide as you realign your stencil. After you are finished stenciling, these tiny dots of paint are then removed with water or paint thinner.

The preparation work you do before you apply your stencil is the key to a good finish. Decide where the border is going to run; it can be either butted right up against the ceiling, using the edge of the stencil as the guideline, or dropped down a length by drawing a line around your room. The space between the ceiling line and the border must be equidistant even if your ceiling line is not straight, as your eye will immediately be drawn to any discrepancies.

PERFECT HORIZONTAL CORNERS

Working into or around corners can be difficult, because as you bend your stencil to fit into the corner and push in your brush, you will often apply too much paint, or smudge your work. To make a neat job, bend your stencil around the corner, using low-tack masking tape, then mask off the part of the stencil that is sitting on the new wall and fill in the pattern just up to the corner of the now-bordered wall. Remove the stencil and tape, and let the paint dry completely. Then, replace the stencil and this time mask off the finished pattern and fill in the cutout that is sitting on the new wall.

PIVOTAL CORNERS

If your border is going to run horizontally along the ceiling and then vertically down the wall, or around the perimeter of a panel, it's important to plan how you want the pattern to change direction. An indistinct pattern such as vines or flowers can run off and start again at the corner pivot point. But for more structured patterns, such as geometric or architectural stencils, a little fudging can go a long way. Before you start, measure the stencil repeats so that you have a good idea where the last pattern repeat will meet the corner. Then, adjust the spacing between repeats to fit your measurements. Alternately, many stencil designs come with **corner stencils,** and for more intricate designs, it's worth paying a little more to get a professional finish.

MATCHING START TO FINISH

It's unlikely that your repeat pattern will match up when you have worked around the room and reached the starting point. If you have chosen a design that must match up, such as an architectural molding, before you start, stencil a few repeats on a sheet of paper, measure the stencil, and divide it into the length of the border. This will let you know how "off" you are going to be if you stick to positioning the stencil around the room exactly as instructed. Once you know the amount of space that will be left over, work that into your calculations to make up the difference. As you move around the room, make very minimal adjustments by positioning the stenciled images a fraction further apart. It's also a good idea to start your border in the least visible part of the room, so that the start and finish points go unnoticed.

OPPOSITE: *A 15-inch-deep checkered border, stamped in apple green, tops lilac-sponged walls in this youthful space. The border adds dimension and interest to the otherwise boxy room.*

gesso border

A raised or an embossed stenciled border is an elaborate alternative to a painted stencil. It's less expensive than adding wood or plaster molding, but it still creates a three-dimensional surface. Choose your design carefully, because many patterns are not suitable for this sophisticated look. Stencils with a linear pattern or a very small design don't work well, but bold, clean patterns are perfect.

This classic design, stenciled with ornamental gesso, contributes to the elegant look of the living room. Although ordinary plaster can be used, the gesso produces a smoother and silkier finish. Here, the natural white of the gesso complements the light frescoed walls. The gesso can be precolored in pastel shades, or the embossed design can be rubbed with color to add to the relief work.

PAINT, PLASTER, AND TOOLS

Base coat
pale gray latex paint, satin
roller, brush, paint tray

Plastered finish
stencil
pencil, ruler
spray adhesive
ornamental gesso (see Resources,
page 190) or plaster
2 plasterer's trowels or spatulas
bucket of water, sponge
Q-tips (if needed)

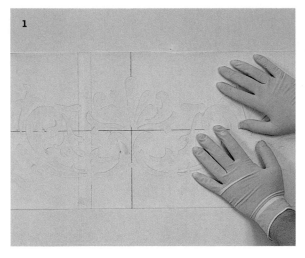

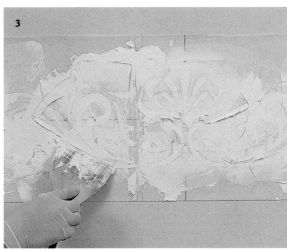

Because the stencil must be washed each time it's used, it's a good idea to have two—while one stencil is drying, you can use the other to continue the pattern. Stenciling with plaster is a job that cannot be rushed, but the results speak for themselves.

INSTRUCTIONS

Prepare your surface following the instructions on page 14. Apply 2 coats of the base coat and let dry for 4 hours. Here, the base coat is a grayish off-white, so the pure white gesso will stand out. Gesso can also be tinted to the desired color (see page 28).

STEP 1: Make registration marks on your stencil and on the wall around the border to ensure that the pattern will be straight. Spray-glue and position the stencil onto the wall, then press it into place. You cannot use tape, because it is essential that the stencil lie perfectly flat.

STEP 2: Place the gesso on a wide trowel or spatula. Lift small amounts onto a smaller spatula. Carefully apply smears of gesso over the stencil. The thicker you apply it, the more the pattern will stand out from the wall; but if it's too thick, the stencil will be difficult to remove from the wall.

STEP 3: Smooth out the gesso so it is even. Periodically wash off the spatula to remove any dried gesso.

STEP 4: Remove the stencil carefully. If any gesso has leaked underneath it, remove the gesso with a Q-tip while it is still wet, or wait until it is dry and sand it off. Wash and dry the stencil immediately, then repeat the stenciling process going around the room.

french country border

Relaxing colors combined with comfortable furnishings and quality linens project an air of quiet elegance in this bedroom tucked under the eaves of a large house, making it a delight to decorate. The shape of the walls inspired me to create a visual impact by hand-painting a vine border where the lower wall meets the sloping ceiling. A strié effect (see page 70) was first painted over the cream base coat on the lower wall in a deep blue, and a 2-inch stripe in the same solid color divides the two walls. A simple vine was then traced along the border overlapping the cream ceiling and blue strié walls. The leaves and stem were painted in an opaque, dove gray blue and then a gold vein was added with transfer foil to highlight each leaf. The monochromatic colors and the delicate shimmer of the vine border emphasize the romantic shape of this French Country bedroom.

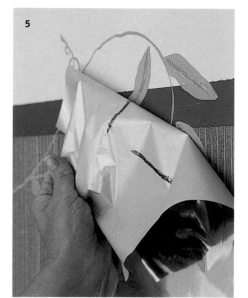

INSTRUCTIONS

STEP 1: Draw or trace a pattern of vines or leaves on a length of paper. This is easy to do free-hand. (Tape 2 or 3 sheets of paper together if you don't have one long enough.) The pattern should repeat itself every few feet, and be deep enough to run over and under the dividing line between ceiling and wall, approximately 8" to 10". Add registration marks where the pattern repeats (see page 95). Lay a strip of waxed paper over your pattern, waxy side up, and trace the pattern and registration marks onto the waxed paper with a pencil. Now, with low-tack masking tape, hold the waxed paper design in place, with the pencil side against the wall. Retrace along the lines, transferring the pencil marks from the back of the waxed paper to the wall. Remove the waxed paper and reposition it along the wall, lining up the registration marks to keep the border straight. Repeat the tracing step on the back of the waxed paper when the pencil marks begin to wear off.

STEP 2: With an artists' brush, paint over the vines and leaves, covering the lines. Fill in the pattern with the gray paint. Let dry thoroughly for 4 hours.

STEP 3: To make the gold vein, paint a line with the gold size through the middle of each leaf. The size goes on white and dries clear. Let dry until tacky, about 5 minutes.

STEP 4: Lay the gold transfer foil, gold side facing you, over a group of the leaves, and rub over the size lines with your finger or a blunt object.

STEP 5: Remove the transfer paper and the gold will be left behind.

NOTE: Except for the size, the wall surface must be completely dry, as the gold transfer will adhere to any sticky or wet area.

PAINT AND TOOLS

Base coat
cream latex paint, satin
roller, brush, paint tray

Painted finish
sharp knife
kitchen sponges
glue
stirring stick
Moroccan red, blue, and leaf
green latex paint, satin
2" paintbrushes, one for each color

casablanca tiled border

A border doesn't necessarily have to circle the room. It can be used in many ways to high-light interesting architectural details. I wanted to feature the splendid paneled white doors in this otherwise plain bedroom. First, I ragged the walls with a sand-colored glaze over the white base coat, leaving an 8-inch plain band of the base coat around the doors. Then, I stamped a border of 2-inch colored squares to simulate the look of old Moroccan tiles. To speed up the process, I glued four squares of kitchen sponge onto one side of a painter's stir-ring stick, painted each sponge a different color, then pressed the squares against the wall to transfer the image. I completed this room with a row of stenciled design around the stamped border.

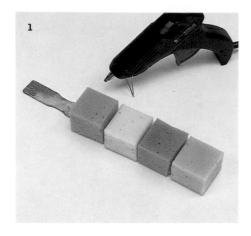

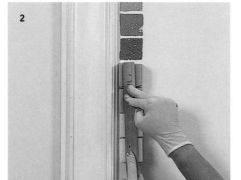

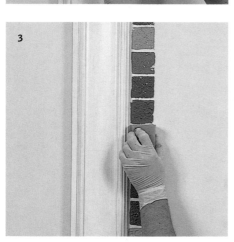

INSTRUCTIONS

Prepare your surface following the instructions on page 14. Apply 2 coats of the base coat and let dry for 4 hours.

STEP 1: Cut four 2" squares from kitchen sponges and glue along one side of the stirring stick, leaving a ¼-inch gap between sponges.

STEP 2: Apply the paint directly onto the exposed surface of the sponges using a brush; alternate the colors. Create a pattern around the door frame by pressing the sponges onto the surface.

STEP 3: Use individual loose sponges to add more paint to a square if the imprint is not strong enough. Remember, you are trying to reproduce old tile, so the squares should not be completely solid.

NOTE: If you come to the end of a row and the premade stamp does not fit, use an individual spare sponge cut to size to complete the border.

lincrusta border

Lincrusta is a heavy embossed wallcovering that was used extensively in England by the Victorians and is now enjoying a revival in North America (see Lincrusta, page 31). It's an ideal solution for walls that have no moldings—it's less expensive than new plaster moldings but does cost more than a wallpaper border. Because of its expense, it is perfect to use as a border in an entrance or hallway, an area where you don't need a great deal of it and a place where it can be easily seen and admired.

A square central hallway in a 1940s apartment was given a dramatic touch with elegant coffee and cream stripes and a painted Lincrusta border. The white doors and trim open up the space and make the space less austere. The Adams-style border was given a coat of copper colored metallic paint and then a verdigris finish.

Lincrusta can be found in good decorating stores in a variety of patterns and widths. It is designed to be decorated once it's in place, either with a solid coat of paint or with a painted finish. See page 32 for instructions on how to apply a Lincrusta border.

Verdigris is the weathered effect that occurs naturally on copper and bronze. Rather than waiting for Mother Nature, you can create the same finish more quickly by using paint. Although I used the finish here on the Lincrusta border, the same technique can be used on any surface. Try it on terra-cotta pots, on bookshelves, or even on walls—the effect will always be stunning. And you can control the amount of verdigris you put on, unlike Mother Nature's finish.

INSTRUCTIONS

Prepare your surface following the instructions on page 14.

STEP 1: Follow the instructions carefully for attaching the Lincrusta to the wall (see page 32). Once it is in place and the glue has fully dried, apply 1 coat of oil-based primer. Let dry.

STEP 2: Apply 2 coats of the copper base coat to the Lincrusta and let dry for four hours.

STEP 3: Using a 3" brush, apply the dark aqua paint randomly over the border, making sure the color goes into all the crevices. Leave to dry.

STEP 4: Repeat the same process, but sparingly, using the light aqua paint; let dry until tacky.

STEP 5: Spray or dab water over the entire surface; let it eat through the drying paints. With a rag, dab over the surface, removing most of the aqua paints and leaving the excess in the indentations of the Lincrusta. Spray with water as needed. The copper base color should be prevalent.

STEP 6: To add to the natural patina, use a rag to dust the surface very lightly with a small amount of white paint.

stenciled silhouettes

The use of silhouettes as framed pictures was popular with the Victorians. In this sophisticated family den, I added a humorous touch by stenciling a border of the silhouettes of each family member, including the pet dog. This effect is an interesting alternative to traditional family portraits.

This room already had a plate rail about 16 inches down from the ceiling. If yours doesn't, you can easily create your own by using tape or a new molding (see page 79).

The base coat was painted in a rich russet red; then cream-colored circles were painted around the border. For the silhouettes, I gathered photographs of the profiles of each family member, then enlarged them on a photocopier to fit inside each circle. I traced the shapes onto Mylar, cut them out, then stenciled them onto the wall in the same color as the base coat.

INSTRUCTIONS

Prepare your surface following the instructions on page 14. Apply 2 coats of the base coat and let dry for 4 hours.

STEP 1: You will need a circular stencil that fits neatly within the confines of the border, and a stencil of the profile of each member of the family. To make the profile stencils, choose pictures, then enlarge them on a photocopier so that each one fits within the circle. Trace each image onto a sheet of Mylar with a marking pen, then cut it out with an X-acto knife. With the marker, draw registration points on the top, bottom, and sides of each stencil so you can position the silhouettes straight on the wall.

STEP 2: Spray the back of the circle stencil with adhesive, then position it on the border.

STEP 3: With a roller, fill in the circle with the cream latex paint. You may need 2 coats to cover the red basecoat. Reposition the stencil and continue making circles around the room. Let dry.

STEP 4: With spray adhesive, position the image stencil inside the dry, cream-painted circle. Using a roller and the russet paint (the wall color) fill in the profile.

STEP 5: Carefully remove the stencil and wipe off any leaks. Let dry.

PAINT AND TOOLS

Base coat
russet red latex paint, satin
roller, brush, paint tray

Painted finish
small roller, paint tray
cream and russet red latex paint, satin
pencil or chalk, ruler

Stencils
photograph of image
tracing paper
Mylar
marking pen
X-acto knife
spray adhesive

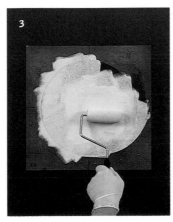
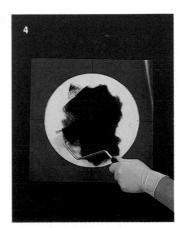

floors

Of all the decorating dilemmas we face, refinishing floors is probably the most challenging, because floors must meet stringent standards. They must be extradurable to withstand the constant pressures of feet and furniture. They must be easy to care for, because cleaning floors, unlike walls, is a daily or weekly necessity. They must be kept in good repair to ensure a safe and healthy environment—free of splinters, nails, loose boards, mold, and mildew. In addition to all this, they should look good. Add to the list that the room must be emptied temporarily while you are laying or decorating a floor, and finally, plan on spending time on your knees.

But the effort is worth it, because a floor finish that's done well underscores the entire room's appeal. If the room is plain, you might decide to make the floor the main feature.

Floors are an area where inspiration and planning are all-important, as you are not likely to redo a floor as quickly as you would change other home decor. It's not necessary that the floors throughout the house match. The contrast between materials is often welcome as you move from hardwood to tiles to carpet. The secret is to make the most of what you have.

WHEN TO PAINT WOOD FLOORS

Hardwood floors are beautiful anywhere. They're long-lasting and more forgiving to stand and walk on than concrete or ceramic tile. Rather than resurface a wood floor that's in good condition, you can add detail with paint or stain as a border, or create a special design in the center as a focal point. The key to longevity is to protect your newly decorated floor with three or four coats of varnish.

A new, unsealed wood floor is very porous, and any paint or stain applied will sink into the wood, yielding translucent coverage that allows the natural graining and knotholes to show through. This is a good way to add some color without losing the inherent beauty of the wood.

Old wood floors have a certain character, but they're often patched or damaged. This is when a simple coat of opaque paint can be an inexpensive decorating solution. But remember, before you start to prime or base-coat your old floor, you must remove any existing varnish, wax, stain, or dirt with a sander. (See preparation chapter, page 14.)

You can apply patterns to old floors in the same way you would to any surface—masking off shapes, stenciling, or block painting. You will see the cracks between the boards, but this is part of the charm of a painted floor. Wear and tear is less visible on a patterned or textured floor than on one that is finished with opaque paint.

An alternative is to paint directly onto plywood. This is becoming increasingly popular, because good-quality plywood is smooth to work on and inexpensive. There is a variety of different-quality plywoods that are ideal to decorate. (In new homes, subfloors may be particleboard, which is usually not suitable for painting.)

A plywood floor must be prepared in the same way as a hardwood floor. The only difference is that because of the limited size of the sheets, you will have several seams, depending on the size of the room. These seams

OPPOSITE: *Painted black and white floors are always a favorite. Here the diamond pattern creates a runner along the hallway.*

must first be filled with caulk, then sanded well, primed, and given a base coat before you apply a finish. Then the finish must be protected with 3 to 4 coats of varnish.

PAINTING CONCRETE FLOORS

Painting directly onto concrete floors is not a new idea, but the concept has taken a leap in style. As wall-to-wall carpet has become less popular, we are all finding new ways of working with the basics, taking what's already there and simply improving its appearance. Concrete floors are not limited to basements. New condominiums are usually built with concrete floors; it's the buyers' choice how they are finished—wall-to-wall carpet, hardwood, tile, or not at all. If you choose concrete, you can paint patterns directly onto the floor, then add area rugs. There are special paints for concrete, and now there are a variety of chemical stains that are used to recreate any authentic stone finish on a floor. In the future we will be seeing these stains used with great imagination in residential homes.

PAINTING OVER LINOLEUM FLOORS

Linoleum is a tough, long-lasting floor material that is warm, softer than wood, and comfortable to walk on—characteristics that make it popular for kitchens and bathrooms. Often it outlasts its visual appeal. As a temporary face-lift, paint can be applied over linoleum, although the finish will not stand up to heavy wear and tear over a long period of time. The trick is to wash and rough up the old linoleum's shiny, durable surface enough so that the painted finish will adhere.

You can have fun painting over an old linoleum floor with faux tiles, border designs, even a faux carpet. Do not, however, try to paint over a cushioned-linoleum floor. The movement in this material as you walk on it will immediately crack the painted finish.

Pieces of linoleum can be cut and painted, then used in the same way that floorcloths are used. It's like painting your own rug on the floor. Loose linoleum lies flatter than a floorcloth and, unlike an entire painted linoleum floor, can be taken with you when you move.

RIGHT: *Concrete can be tinted with special chemical stains to create a permanent, translucent colored finish for interior use as well as outside statuaries, ornaments, pool decks, and driveways. See Distributors, page 191, for information on where to find the products.*

PAINT AND TOOLS

Base coat
off-white latex paint, satin
roller, brush, paint tray

Painted finish
cardboard
pencil, ruler
sharp knife
Mylar
chalk line
sand and caramel latex paint, satin
stencil brush
varnish

Top coat
yellow ocher artists' acrylic

honeycomb floor

No one has ever entered this hallway without commenting on the honeycomb pattern on
the floor. Although it took some time to measure and plan, and caused a little wear and tear
on the knees, it was well worth it—the final effect is stunning. The floor was stripped of
years of old varnish and stain, then primed and painted with a cream base coat, the light-
est of the three colors used. I made a hexagonal template to trace the pattern, then two diamond stencils to add the second and third sandy tones. I tinted the protective varnish with
yellow ocher to produce the final honey glow. Because this exquisite design takes time, it
might be best to limit it to a small area, such as an entrance hall or even a dining room
tabletop or screen.

INSTRUCTIONS

Prepare your surface following the instructions on page 14. Apply 1 coat of the base coat and let dry for 4 hours.

STEP 1: Cut out a cardboard template with 6 sides, the 2 top and 2 bottom sides each measuring $4\frac{1}{4}$". The remaining 2 sides should each be 4". This hexagon is used as a template to make the honeycomb design. It is made up of 3 diamonds (parallelograms). Cut 2 Mylar diamond stencils, one 4" $\times$ $4\frac{1}{4}$" and one $4\frac{1}{4}$" $\times$ $4\frac{1}{4}$", that will fit into the hexagon.

STEP 2: Apply diagonal guidelines across the floor with a chalk line to keep your design straight. Position the hexagon template on the floor and trace around it with a pencil. Pick up the template, move it to the next position with the side points touching, and trace again. Repeat until the pattern covers the floor.

STEP 3: Place the first diamond stencil into position in the hexagon and fill in with sand latex paint. A stencil brush is best to minimize leakage under the stencil. Repeat for all hexagons. Let dry.

STEP 4: Position the second diamond stencil and fill in with caramel latex. Repeat for all hexagons. Let dry.

STEP 5: Add a small amount of yellow ocher tint to some of the varnish to make a rich honey color. A total of 4 coats of varnish are needed for adequate protection, but only the first coat should be tinted.

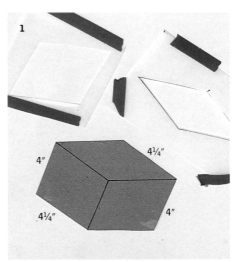

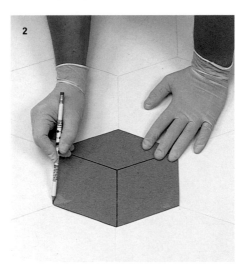

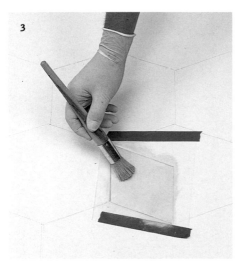

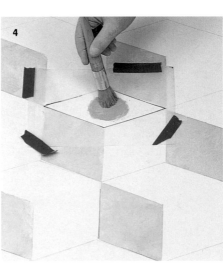

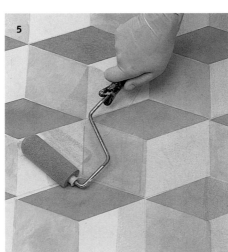

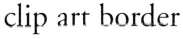

RECIPE

1 part latex paint
1 part water-based glazing liquid

PAINT AND TOOLS

Base coat
cream latex paint, satin
roller, brush, paint tray

Painted finish
yellow ocher and
pistachio latex paint, satin
water-based glazing liquid
mixing containers
pencil, ruler
chalk line
low-tack masking tape
clean, soft rags
motifs (clip art)
carbon or transfer paper
pencil or ballpoint pen
artists' brush
small amount of gray latex paint
indelible green marking pen
varnish

clip art border

New modern kitchens afford us the luxury of updated appliances and functional fixtures, but they are often sterile. You probably don't want to touch your new cupboards or countertops, so a good way to add warmth to this room is on the walls and floor. Here I colorwashed the walls in a soft pistachio green. Instead of laying tile on the floor, plywood was used. It was cut to shape, installed, then sanded, primed, and given a base coat of off-white paint. Then the whole surface was colorwashed roughly in a yellow ocher glaze, and a 5-inch border was masked off and ragged in pistachio green.

The irregular shape of the kitchen is accented by the border, giving character to an otherwise ordinary space. Motifs taken from clip art were hand-painted over the border. These designs can be taken off a computer or copied out of a clip art illustration book. There are thousands to choose from, and they can be reduced or enlarged to the appropriate size on a photocopier. To highlight the motifs, I outlined each one with a marking pen.

As with all floors, three to four coats of varnish should be applied to protect the finish.

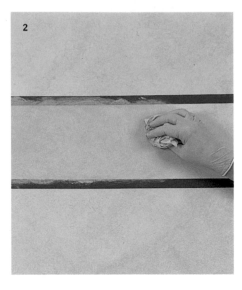

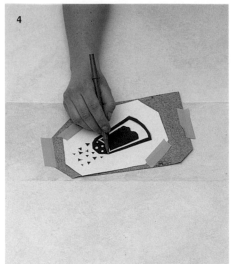

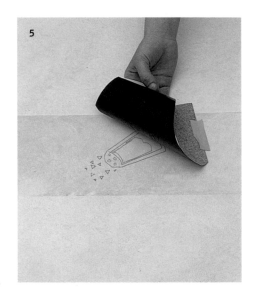

INSTRUCTIONS

Prepare your surface following the instructions on page 14. Apply 1 coat of the base coat and let dry for 4 hours.

STEP 1: Prepare the glazes. Colorwash the floor with yellow ocher (see page 53 for instructions) and let dry.

STEP 2: With a pencil, ruler, and chalk line, mark a 5" border and mask it off. Use the same color-washing technique to fill in the border with the pistachio glaze.

STEP 3: Photocopy an image to a size that will fit neatly inside the border.

STEP 4: Cut a piece of carbon paper to size and lay it between the border and the image. Draw around the image to transfer it to the floor.

STEP 5: Remove the image and carbon paper; the design will now be transferred to the floor.

STEP 6: With an artists' brush and gray paint, hand-paint the image.

NOTE: Use a green marking pen to highlight around the image. Make sure the marker is indelible, or it will bleed when you apply the varnish. Protect the finish with 4 coats of varnish; let cure completely, about 4 days.

block painting

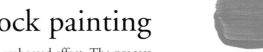

Block painting is a technique that produces a hand-painted, embossed effect. The process is less elaborate than stenciling, but the end result is often more realistic. Designs are made using precut pieces of soft rubber with score marks etched into the surface, such as the veined leaf we used here. Paint or tinted glaze is lightly brushed onto the scored surface, then the pad is pressed into place on the wall or floor. See page 25 for instructions and tips on block painting.

Block painting can be used on most painted surfaces. In this quaint loft, a diamond pattern was mapped out over a moss green base coat, then the rubber leaf was pressed along the lines.

The topiary on the wall was applied using the same block painting kit. A disposable planting pot was cut in half and glued directly onto the bottom of the tree. The addition of real Spanish moss to the pot adds to the charm of this fanciful garden room.

INSTRUCTIONS

Prepare your surface following the instructions on page 14. Apply 2 coats of the base coat and let dry for 4 hours.

STEP 1: Map out a diamond grid with a chalk line (see page 33 for instructions) The diamonds should be 14" across.

STEP 2: Brush dark green glaze onto the side of the rubber leaf pad that has veins cut into it. Hold the rubber pad by its handle and press it onto the floor, using the chalk line as a guide. Lift the pad, then press it down again. Repaint the pad after 3 or 4 presses, because the impression starts to fade. By following the pencil marks, a diamond pattern of leaves is created.

STEP 3: Apply a small red dot to the corners of each diamond by dipping the eraser end of a pencil into glaze and pressing it onto the surafce. Let the paint dry completely before you wipe off the chalk lines.

STEP 4: Apply 4 coats of varnish to protect the finish; let cure completely, about 4 days, before moving furniture back into the room.

PAINT AND TOOLS

Base coat
moss green latex paint, satin
roller, brush, paint tray

Painted finish
pencil, ruler
chalk line
block painting kit (comes with rubber
pads and colored glaze) *or* mix latex
paint and a little water-based glazing
liquid to make your own colors
pencil with tip eraser
varnish and brush

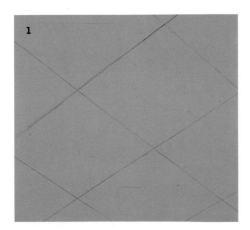

RECIPE

1 part latex paint
1 part water-based glazing liquid

PAINT AND TOOLS

Base coat
cream latex paint, satin
roller, brush, paint tray

Painted finish
pencil, ruler
chalk line
½" low-tack masking tape
apricot and aqua latex paint, satin
water-based glazing liquid
mixing containers
2" foam brush
clean, soft rags
small piece of chicken wire
4" paintbrush
paper towel
varnish and brush

cottage floor

A plywood floor is like a blank artists' canvas: It allows you to be as creative as you please. In this rustic cottage, the floors were primed and given a base coat of cream paint. Then apricot and aqua glazes were ragged over alternate diamonds to produce a faded finish. Because we masked out the diamond pattern using ½-inch tape, we were able to apply both colors at the same time, making this a quick and easy job. Always remove low-tack tape from a freshly painted floor immediately, and very carefully.

The best part of this floor is the border. With the help of a friend, I held down a strip of chicken wire while my partner brushed over the surface with a small amount of paint and a very dry brush; then we lifted the wire. The resulting pattern makes a fabulous border.

INSTRUCTIONS

Prepare your surface following the instructions on page 14. Apply 2 coats of the base coat and let dry overnight.

STEP 1: Map out a diamond grid with a chalk line (see page 33 for instructions). Leave an 8" border around the edge. Center the tape over the chalk line and press it into place. Once the tape is removed, this line will be the space around the diamonds.

STEP 2: Prepare the glazes. Brush the apricot glaze onto alternate diamonds.

STEP 3: Crumple a rag and pat it over the glaze to soften it and add texture. Let dry completely.

STEP 4: In the same manner, fill in and texture the rest of the diamonds with the aqua glaze.

STEP 5: Remove the tape, wipe out the chalk line, and let dry.

STEP 6: Cut the chicken wire slightly wider than the border, about 9 inches. Tape or staple the wire into place. Dip a 4" brush into a small amount of the aqua paint, wipe any excess onto a paper towel, and dry-brush loosely over the wire. Build up the color as desired.

STEP 7: Remove the wire and let the paint dry completely. Apply 4 coats of varnish for protection, then let the floor cure completely, about 4 days, before moving any furniture back in.

OPPOSITE: *The flip side of an outdated carpet runner in this hallway proved to be an inexpensive alternative to sisal. A simple border was stenciled with latex paint, and the result is a perfect complement to the lively walls and door.*

ceilings

Ceilings are the most difficult areas of a room to paint, both physically and from a creative perspective, so we often resort to a simple coat of white throughout the house, then move on to the walls.

However, ceilings in small areas such as a bathroom, a child's bedroom, or an entrance hall aren't intimidating, and a special effect here can add greatly to the room's character. Attic ceilings that slope over and around windows, or meet the walls as low as 2 to 3 feet from the floor, offer another unique opportunity for creative painting. If there are so many angles that it's hard to know where to start and stop the wall and ceiling finishes, apply a single painted finish over all the surfaces to unite them.

In older homes without moldings, the break line between the ceiling and the walls is often marred with small cracks and chips, bumpy plaster, or a poor seam. You will find it impossible to paint a clean edge unless you drop the break line down an inch or two away from the uneven seam. The other alternative is to ignore the uneven edge and add an eye-catching border.

A ceiling that is badly cracked or crumbling from water damage must be attended to before fresh paint is applied. Special primers will cover up water stains after they have dried completely if the surface material has not been permanently damaged. A paint or plaster technique will help camouflage less than perfect repairs. This is why stucco ceilings are so popular with contractors and landlords, however. They are usually loathed by homeowners. I'm constantly asked what can be done to enliven stucco ceilings. The first option is to com-pletely remove the stucco—a huge, messy, and expensive job. The second option is to just ignore the ceiling and make the rest of your surroundings as beautiful as possible. A simple colorwash over a relatively smooth stucco ceiling will help a little; it won't be effective on the icing sugar type of stucco.

WHITE IS RIGHT

Although general rules govern when a ceiling should be colored or remain white, ultimately it depends on the overall mood you set out to establish.

In rooms that have high ceilings, moldings at the top of the walls, and/or plaster medallions on the ceiling, I recommend painting the entire surface cream or off-white. If you have interesting ceiling moldings, apply the white in a semigloss sheen. The surface needs no other embellishment; it acts as a fresh counterpoint to whatever wall covering you choose.

Add color to a ceiling when you want to create a cozy or an intimate mood. A ceiling with a dark color or painted finish will feel lower than if it is plain white and is an ideal treatment for small Victorian rooms. Besides, a white ceiling against dark walls is too jarring a contrast. If you do paint a room a dark color, use a lighter tone of the wall color or a cream color on the ceiling to give a classic finish.

SLOPED CEILINGS

Simple painted finishes and a judicious use of borders will solve the problem of awkward ceiling breaks in attic spaces and rooms with dormers. A sponged or ragged

moroccan bathroom

This magnificent tent ceiling was achieved with paint and patience. Working from a roman shade of striped fabric, I copied the design onto the walls using blue and green glazes matched to the material. I then painted dentils over alternating stripes just like the real fabric dentils over the blinds. As a finishing touch, real tassels were attached with upholstery tacks to each point. To create the illusion of fabric gathered into the center of the ceiling, the stripes were painted to gather into the ceiling fixture.

painted finish applied to ceilings and walls will uncomplicate the room's architecture. Run a border along the lines you choose to emphasize, such as around windows and doors and following major seams or wall breaks. Painting oddly shaped rooms may seem like a challenge at first, but they often end up with the most character and become favorite spaces in which to spend time.

SMALL IS BEAUTIFUL

Take advantage of the diminutive size of a bathroom ceiling to do something special. This is the place to apply more costly materials, such as gold leaf, metallic paints, and finishes that take a lot of time. You could treat the ceiling and the walls to a simple faux marble finish, or add a stenciled border detail that flows up and over the ceiling and around a mirror, window, or door. Because the room is small, details will be seen and enjoyed, so it's worth adding elaborate touches.

TIPS FOR: *painting ceilings*

1. Use a safe ladder, or erect scaffolding if the job is big.

2. To get a clean edge between wall and ceiling, tape off approximately ½" below the ceiling along the wall, and continue the ceiling paint down to this line.

3. To catch drips from your roller or brush, attach a piece of cardboard to the top of the handle, underneath the bristles or sponge.

4. Ceiling paint has a flat finish and is porous. Although it's less expensive than paint manufactured for walls, it's ideal for ceilings. The standard matte finish diminishes visibility of minor cracks and bumps. Never use ceiling paint on walls.

5. You cannot apply a colored glaze over ceiling paint, as the glaze will be absorbed into the surface with disastrous results.

6. If you intend to put a special paint finish on the ceiling, first prime, and then with regular paint, apply one or two coats of the base color.

RECIPE

1 part latex paint
1 part water-based glazing liquid

PAINT AND TOOLS

Primer base coat
bronze latex paint
2″ paintbrush

Painted finish
bronze latex paint
water-based glazing liquid
mixing container
small amount of black latex paint
stippling brush or
hard-bristle paintbrush
clean, soft rags

bronzed moldings

The walls in this classic study have a lustrous russet brown faux leather finish (see page 63), and I wanted something equally luxurious to complement the effect. Here was the perfect place to use metallic paint, which produces an opulent, mellow glow.

Metallic paints are currently fashionable and are available as bronze, silver, gold, or copper powders that you mix into a glaze. More and more dealers also sell them ready-mixed. For this ceiling, I chose a dark silvery green that blends well with the tone on the walls. Two coats were applied with a roller. Generally, a dark shade will pull the ceiling down, but for a cozy den such as this, the deep colors helped to create just the right mood.

The moldings in the room are the original ornate plaster that have been painted over many times. I made them even more beautiful by applying bronze paint, then rubbing them with a dark bronze glaze, which highlighted the relief work. I added a ceiling medallion as well. These medallions, which are available at decorating stores, are made of wood, plaster, or styrofoam. The one I chose looked too new alongside the old Victorian moldings, so I antiqued it using bronze paint as the base coat and a darker bronze glaze stippled over the surface. To highlight the carved details, I gently rubbed the surface with a rag, leaving the dark bronze glaze behind in the crevices. The medallion now looks like a vintage piece and matches the rest of the moldings.

INSTRUCTIONS

Prepare your surface following the instructions on page 14.

STEP 1: Prime the medallion.

STEP 2: Apply 1 coat of the base coat and let dry for 4 hours.

STEP 3: Mix some of the bronze paint with the glazing liquid, then add a small amount of black paint to the glaze. With a brush, apply this darker bronze glaze over the base coat, making sure it reaches all the crevices. If you're working along a length of molding, apply the glaze in 3' sections so the glaze stays wet enough to be manipulated.

STEP 4: When the bronze glaze becomes tacky, wipe a folded rag gently over the surface, removing some of the glaze but leaving most of it behind in the crevices. Do not let the glaze become too tacky or it will be hard to rub off.

gold leaf ceiling

Gilding is a highly specialized art form traditionally used on ornamental relief work. Fine sheets of real gold leaf are normally used in this craft, but nowadays a less expensive imitation dutch metal gold leaf is commonly used. It can be applied in a variety of ways and on many unconventional surfaces.

Gilding a large ceiling is a huge and expensive job, but the ceiling of this small powder room was a perfect candidate for this technique. The glorious checkerboard pattern of gold leaf and gold metallic paint transformed the room from an ordinary space into an extraordinary one, at little cost.

Gold leaf is usually applied to the surface over gold size, a sticky varnish designed specifically for this purpose. But because this ceiling would not be subjected to any wear and tear, I chose not to use the gold size varnish. Instead, I invented an easier way to apply the gold leaf, using a homemade applicator and the still-tacky gold base coat as an adhesive. It took a little practice to get the gold leaf squares in the proper position, but the luminous effect was worth the effort.

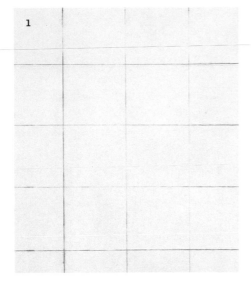

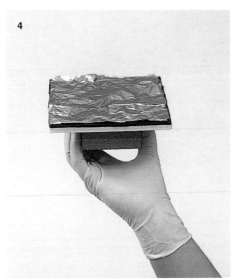

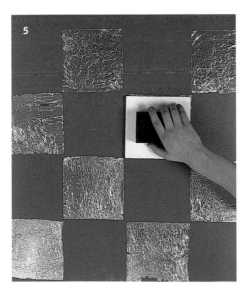

INSTRUCTIONS

Prepare your surface following the instructions on page 14. To make the gold leaf applicator, cut a piece of foam core or Masonite the same size as a sheet of gold leaf (approximately 4" square). Glue the foam core to a sanding sponge or a block of wood, then glue a piece of velvet or felt to the top of the foam core. The gold leaf, which is extremely thin and delicate, will cling to the fabric, allowing you to stamp it carefully into place on the ceiling.

STEP 1: With a partner, map out a grid of 4" squares (the size of a piece of gold leaf) with a chalk line.

STEP 2: In the corner of each square, make a tiny hole with a pushpin. These are your registration marks for the gold leaf.

STEP 3: Apply 1 or 2 coats of the base coat over the ceiling and let dry until tacky.

STEP 4: Eliminate drafts when you are applying the gold leaf by closing any windows or heating vents, and turning off fans. Lay a sheet of gold leaf onto the velvet side of the applicator.

STEP 5: Carefully move the applicator to the ceiling, line up the gold leaf between the 4 pinholes, and press it gently into place on the tacky paint. If the sheet does not go on straight, remove what you can, let the base coat dry, then sand off any remaining gold leaf. Fill in this square later with a small amount of base coat, then reapply the gold leaf. Continue to apply gold leaf to every other square, creating a checkerboard pattern.

NOTE: If the gold leaf does not go on completely solid, fill in any gaps with a small amount of leaf applied to a dry brush.

RIGHT: *This vestibule ceiling has been sponged in stone colors to complement the stone-blocked walls. Lighter tones were sponged on first and then darker stone colors were flicked over the surface with a stiff brush. The effect is carried over the moldings to meet the walls, rather than painting the moldings separately, making fewer breaks in a small space.*

RECIPE

1 part latex paint
1 part water-based glazing liuqid

PAINT AND TOOLS

Base coat
white latex paint, satin
bristle brush, split-foam roller

Painted finish
ocher latex paint, satin
water-based glazing liquid
mixing container
3" or 4" hard-bristle brush
or a wallpaper brush

distressed stucco ceiling

Stucco can be applied in many different textured patterns, from smooth or lightly textured designs to the sharp, pointy icing sugar finishes often seen on ceilings. I generally leave these pointy ceilings white, and draw the eye away to more interesting walls and furnishings, but it is possible to decorate them. There are few finishes that can be applied to a stucco ceiling, but colorwashing is a good option for this uneven surface.

Colorwashing on stucco is physically more demanding than on a smooth surface. If the stucco is pointy, use a brush instead of a rag. Use very little paint and apply it in a tight crisscross motion, working the colored glaze into the creases and crevices of the plaster.

The rounded corners of this curved ceiling were architecturally more pleasing than a typical flat one. The walls have been frottaged in a rich red, leaving the stark white ceiling very prominent, but with the application of a soft ocher colorwash the ceiling now blends in with the flavor of the room.

INSTRUCTIONS

Prepare your surface following the instructions on page 14.

STEP 1: If the stucco has been painted with ceiling paint, apply a base coat of latex paint to prevent the glaze from being absorbed. Let dry for 4 hours.

STEP 2: Prepare the glaze. With a wide-bristle brush, apply the glaze using crisscross strokes, working it into the crevices of the stucco. Go over some areas more than others, graduating the amount of color to create a distressed appearance. Let dry.

RECIPE

2 parts latex paint
2 parts water-based glazing liquid
1 part water

PAINT AND TOOLS

Base coat
cream latex paint, satin
roller, brush, paint tray

Painted finish
sand latex paint, satin
water-based glazing liquid
mixing container
roller, size of desired stripe
raw potatoes
knife
paper towel
small amount of black,
pale yellow, and raw sienna
latex paint or artists' acrylic
¼" artists' brush

leopard ceiling

Nature has given us the most fascinating patterns of all, especially those found on animal skins. They have always been a wonderful source of inspiration for decorating whether for fabrics, carpeting, or even painted finishes. This bedroom ceiling was given a wild touch by stamping the surface with a design cut into a raw potato, much like the potato stamping we all did in kindergarten. When you are trying to reproduce an animal skin, refer to a photograph or a piece of fabric to get an idea of the texture and color found in the real thing.

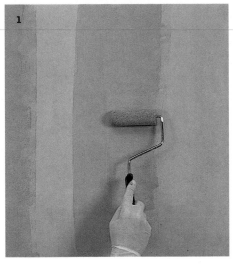

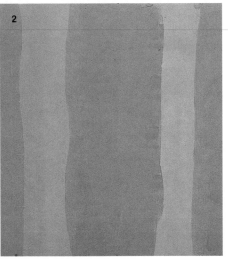

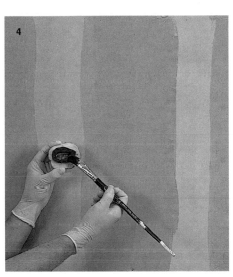

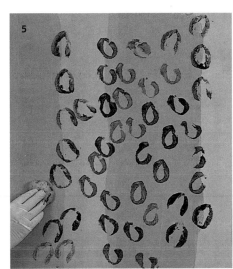

INSTRUCTIONS

Prepare your surface following the instructions on page 14. Apply 2 coats of the base coat and let dry for 4 hours.

STEP 1: Prepare the sand glaze. Roll the glaze in stripes across the ceiling. Here, the stripes are the size of the roller and about 4" apart. They should be slightly irregular, with smudged edges.

STEP 2: Finish the whole ceiling with irregular stripes, then let dry.

STEP 3: To make the stamps for the leopard spots, cut a potato in half, carve an oval shape on the flat end, then carve a hole inside the oval. Wrap the cut potato in a paper towel to absorb excess moisture.

STEP 4: Apply black paint to the oval ring.

STEP 5: Stamp in different directions over the surface. Smudge the images slightly so they resemble fur.

STEP 6: With an artists' brush, fill in the center of most of the black ovals with the pale yellow latex paint. Paint loosely with irregular brush marks.

STEP 7: Add a dot of raw sienna to the pale yellow dots inside the oval.

RECIPE

1 part latex paint
1 part water-based glazing liquid

PAINT AND TOOLS

Base coat
white latex paint, satin
roller, brush, paint tray

Painted finish
light and dark blue latex paint
water-based glazing liquid
mixing containers
4" paintbrushes
white latex paint
2" paintbrush or pointed fitch

cloudy sky

There are many variations in skies and in the methods of replicating a sky with paint. Painted skies can be as realistic as those seen on historic church ceilings painted by famed Italian artists or as simple as a pale blue and white colorwashed surface.

This guest bedroom is a romantic space with sloping gabled walls. I continued the faux sky right down to the baseboards. The walls were first colorwashed in two tones of blue glaze to give a mottled background. The billowy clouds are pure white paint, broken in areas by the addition of more blue. This sky effect is easy to control because it's a process whereby the paint is built up. So if you're not happy with an area or with the shape or density of the clouds, simply add more blue or white paint.

colorwashed sky

The gabled walls in this bathroom have been colorwashed with a soft blue glaze over a cream base coat. The technique is the same as that used on the terra-cotta walls on page 53. Here, the finish is light and whimsical and was much faster to apply than the previous cloudy sky.

INSTRUCTIONS

Prepare your surface following the instructions on page 14. Apply 2 coats of the base coat and let dry for 4 hours.

STEP 1: Prepare the glazes. With a 4" brush, apply the dark blue glaze in crisscross strokes over the surface. Let dry.

STEP 2: Repeat with the light blue glaze over the top, covering about 70% of the surface and creating a mottled look.

STEP 3: To create clouds, outline some of the blue shapes you have created using undiluted white paint and a 2" brush or a fitch. Apply a heavier layer of white paint on the same side of each cloud to simulate where the sunlight is hitting it. Work the rest of the cloud in a soft, swirling motion. You are building the clouds in a billowy pattern with different densities of white paint. To make the clouds realistic, they should all be moving in the same direction, as if blown by the wind.

STEP 4: Keep stepping back from your work to get an overall view. You can add more blue paint to fill in the cloud areas until you're satisfied with the result.

kitchens
and bathrooms

Kitchens and bathrooms are different from other rooms in the house because they are mostly comprised of set furnishings—cabinets, counters, appliances, and fixtures. Because of this, redoing these rooms when the decor becomes outdated can be very costly. You may not be ready to go to the trouble and expense of installing new cabinets, sinks, or countertops, or you may be renting and stuck with what you have. This is where paint becomes your best friend.

Kitchens and bathrooms are ideal spaces for color and decoration. The rooms' different surfaces are ideal for adding extra life with paint. There's a world of resources available to inspire you—stores that specialize in these critical home spaces will give you ideas, as will the multitude of exciting decorating magazines and style books. You will be delighted to discover how easy it is to replicate a luscious-looking row of tiles, or even build a wall of shimmery glass blocks, simply with paint. Accessories and fabrics abound that will help you build on any style or theme. These are the busiest rooms in the home, so they must be practical and easy to keep clean, but they can also be a delightful setting for your favorite designs and memorabilia.

Being in an old or shabby kitchen or bathroom day in and day out can be disheartening. If you're renting or are not ready to renovate, it's time to do what you can with paint. Bronze, copper, gold, and especially silver

paints are popular and fit beautifully into a makeover. Silver as a base coat offers a lovely patina to pastel glazes and is compatible with contemporary appliances and fixtures as well as older ones. Gold is very grand to use as an opulent accent, and affordable for a small area such as a powder room.

The wall and floor coverings used in kitchens and bathrooms are generally hard-wearing and durable veneers, laminates, and ceramic tiles. Their smooth surfaces have been almost impossible to repaint until the advent of today's highly adherent primers. Now, rather than replace aging wall tiles, dated cabinets, and linoleum floors, you can paint these shiny surfaces, as long as you prepare them properly (see page 14). If you are not able to change unattractive features, then divert attention to a fresh painted finish on the walls, doors, cabinets, or even the backsplash area. Create something noteworthy to catch the eye and forget about the cracked counter tile until it can be replaced.

Decorating kitchens and bathrooms can be a challenge, but it can also be satisfying. With such a small area to cover, you can let your imagination take flight and try painted finishes that might otherwise seem daunting. Remember that decorating is supposed to raise your spirits and brighten your life. If you're not pleased with your efforts, try again—it's just a coat of paint.

OPPOSITE: *This tiny powder room has no natural light, but with halogen track lights and a coat of burnt orange stucco, we've created the illusion that the walls are drenched by the Mexican sun. Positioning the washstand so it is angled into the corner helps make the most of the limited space. The walls have been lightly textured with stucco, then sealed and given a coat of terracotta-colored paint.*

kitchen cabinets and backsplashes

OPPOSITE: *In this country kitchen, white tiles were dressed up with a simple country motif using ceramic paints. I sanded the tiles and hand-painted the design. Because the tiles were already attached to the wall and therefore the paint couldn't be heat-set, I gave each tile (not the grouting) 2 coats of varnish to protect the paint.*

Because we spend a great deal of time in the kitchen, it should have a happy, energetic atmosphere—bright, clean, and conducive to cooking, chatting over a cup of coffee, and doing homework. A kitchen with outdated and shabby counters and cupboards is depressing to work in. The assembly-line design of some of today's new kitchens can be just as unwelcoming. But if you are renting, or just starting out in a new home, a major kitchen renovation may not be feasible. You can, however, make a dramatic change to the feel and focus of the kitchen by painting some of its major features—the cupboards, walls, backsplash area, and floor. For a quick and satisfying decorating fix, nothing can update your kitchen as successfully as paint.

In this section, I'll demonstrate how inventive painting can transform your kitchen cabinets and backsplash area. Because the cabinets cover a large amount of wall space, changing their look will have a powerful effect on the whole room.

Countertops take a heavy beating, so I don't recommend painting them. But a new treatment on the backsplash will redirect your eye away from stained or dated counters.

REINVENT KITCHEN CABINETS

Cabinets are made from solid wood, wood veneer, or laminate, all of which are paintable. When deciding on a finish, it's important to consider the shape and style of the cabinet doors and choose a finish that suits that style. Flat-fronted wood or laminate doors provide an unbroken surface, perfect for finishes that require a smooth base, such as wood graining. Aged or distressed finishes look good on cabinet doors with decorative moldings. Cabinets are like pieces of furniture; they do not have to be the same colors as the walls, and a variety of designs can be used to dress them up.

A SPIRITED BACKSPLASH

The backsplash above a kitchen sink or countertop is often overlooked, but it's an excellent surface on which to add an interesting finish—it's at eye level when you're sitting and a focal point when you're standing at the sink. Lighting installed under the cabinets will enhance a new painted finish in this area even more. The backsplash may be made of the same material as your countertop, but it doesn't get the same wear and tear as the counter. Although it needs to be easy to wipe clean, it will never have to withstand a hot pot or a knife blade. Two coats of varnish over the painted finish should be enough to protect it from water or splattered food. Because it's not a big area, you can let your imagination run wild. Paint is less expensive than decorative ceramic tiles, and this is an ideal space for color and pattern. Because the area is so visible, it can take your mind off an uninspired counter or floor.

TIPS FOR: *how to prepare a shiny surface for paint*

Ceramic tile, laminate, and other shiny surfaces can be painted now that special primers have been designed for this purpose.

1. Especially in a kitchen where there's not only dirt but a buildup of grease and smoke, you have to do a little scrubbing before you start or the paint will not adhere. Use a heavy-duty cleanser or vinegar and a scouring pad to cut the grease, then rinse carefully and wipe dry.

2. Shiny, smooth surfaces such as laminates and tile give paint nothing to hang on to. So after cleaning, rough up the surface with sandpaper.

3. Apply a primer that is made specifically to cover high-gloss surfaces. It must be superadherent, which should be specified on the can. Ask your paint or hardware dealer to show you the correct primer for your project.

4. Apply your painted finish.

5. A painted surface in the kitchen should be sealed. Cabinets need 1 coat of varnish, backsplashes 2 coats.

RECIPE

4 parts latex paint
1 part water

PAINT AND TOOLS

Base coat
white latex paint, satin
small roller, brush, paint tray

Painted finish
thick kitchen sponges
or upholstery foam
sharp knife
mint green and indigo
latex paint, satin
mixing containers
paper plates
paper towels

Stencil
Mylar
marking pen
sharp knife
low-tack masking tape
gold size
gold leaf
small, soft brush
oil-based varnish to cover gold leaf
and brush

regal backsplash

The backsplash in this tiny kitchenette is a row of dull ceramic tiles. The eye is drawn away from these tiles by enhancing the wall above them with painted tiles and naive gold leaf crowns. I first applied a white base coat, which acts as the grout lines. I used two 4-inch kitchen sponges to stamp the wall with alternate colors of mint green and indigo, then I stenciled glimmery gold crowns sporadically onto some of the tiles. Instead of paint, I used gold leaf to add pizzazz.

INSTRUCTIONS

Prepare your surface following the instructions on page 14. Apply 2 coats of the base coat and let dry for 4 hours. This base coat will be the color of the grout lines.

STEP 1: Cut two 4" squares from thick kitchen sponges or a piece of upholstery foam. Map out reference points for the tile placement on the backsplash, leaving $\frac{1}{4}$" spaces between the tiles to represent the grout lines (see Measuring, page 32). Thin the green and indigo paints with water. Pour each color onto a separate plate. Working with alternate colors, press the sponge into the paint; dab off the excess on a paper towel, and press onto the surface. Let dry completely.

STEP 2: Cut out a simple Mylar stencil in the shape of a crown. Position the stencil onto a tile with tape. Do not use spray adhesive; it will cause the gold leaf to stick to the wall in areas where you don't want it. Fill in the cutout with the gold size. Adding a small amount of color, any color, to the size will make it more visible on the wall. Remove the stencil and let the gold size become tacky.

STEP 3: Gently lay a sheet of gold leaf over the tacky gold size. Pat it very gently into place with a small, soft brush or a rag. Let the gold size dry completely, about 1 hour.

STEP 4: With the same soft brush, dust away the excess gold leaf. The only leaf that will stay on the surface is the leaf that is stuck to the gold size.

STEP 5: Apply 2 coats of varnish to the backsplash for protection.

fantasy wood graining on cabinets

I gave these plain kitchen cabinets brand-new style with a 1950s color scheme and new chrome handles. A traditional wood-graining effect was applied to the flat-fronted laminate cabinet doors, but instead of using authentic wood colors, I chose bright turquoise. As I pulled a small tool called a rocker through the glaze, its grooves created a pattern of grain and knots that is found in pine.

INSTRUCTIONS

Prepare your surface following the instructions on page 14. Apply 2 coats of the base coat and let dry for 4 hours. Prepare the glaze.

STEP 1: Working on one door at a time and using vertical brush strokes, apply an even coat of the glaze with a 3" brush, covering 100% of the surface.

STEP 2: Hold the rocker like a large pencil and, starting at the top and one edge of the cabinet door, pull down through the glaze, rocking your wrist backward and forward. Go back to the top of the door and pull the rocker through the glaze again, overlapping the previous stroke slightly. Work in vertical strokes until the door is complete.

STEP 3: Because this is a kitchen, protect the finish with one or two coats of varnish.

TIP: Practice with the rocker on a piece of paper or board until you are satisfied with how often you need to rock your wrist to get an authentic-looking pattern. If you want to achieve the look of real knotty pine, first apply a base coat of cream paint, then use a honey-colored glaze coat.

RECIPE

1 part latex paint
1 part water-based glazing liquid

PAINT AND TOOLS

Base coat
light aqua latex paint, satin
roller, brush, paint tray

Painted finish
turquoise latex paint, satin
water-based glazing liquid
mixing container
3" paintbrush
rocker
varnish

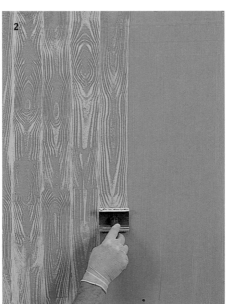

PAINT AND TOOLS

Base coat
red latex paint, satin
roller, brush, paint tray

Painted finish
crackle medium
foam brushes
blue latex paint, satin
varnish and brush

crackle finish cabinets

A tiny cottage kitchen was given a face-lift by applying a crackle finish to the cupboard doors. Crackle paint is one of the most popular techniques for antiquing or distressing surfaces. The effect can be as dramatic or as subtle as required, depending on the colors used and the size of the cracks. Crackle medium can be bought in craft and decorating stores. The price varies immensely; I seem to have the most success with the least expensive brands.

The base coat will be the color of the cracks; the top coat will be the overall color. Between these two layers, a coat of crackle medium is applied. Once this is dry, the top coat is painted on in clean strokes. As the top layer of paint dries, the cracks appear before your eyes. The thicker the top layer of paint, the wider the cracks; the thinner it's applied, the finer the cracks will appear. A crackle surface must always be finished off with at least one coat of varnish for protection.

INSTRUCTIONS

Prepare your surface following the instructions on page 14. Apply 2 coats of the base coat and let dry for 4 hours.

STEP 1: Apply the crackle medium with a foam brush in smooth, even strokes. Do not overwork.

STEP 2: Apply the blue paint in thin, smooth strokes, just like the crackle medium. You will disturb the crackle medium if you go backward and forward too much.

STEP 3: As the paint begins to dry the cracks will appear. Once thoroughly dry, apply 2 coats of varnish to protect your finish.

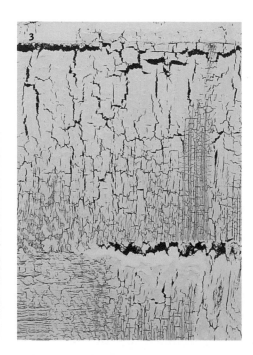

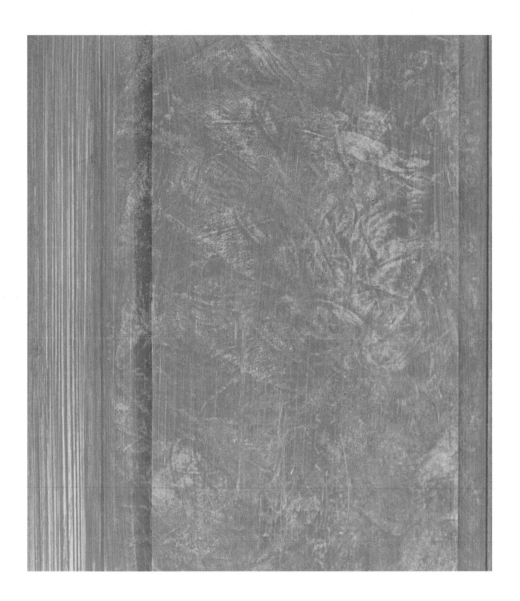

RECIPE

1 part latex paint
1 part water-based glazing liquid

PAINT AND TOOLS

Base coat
cream latex paint
2" or 3" paintbrush

Painted finish
vintage green latex paint, satin
water-based glazing liquid
mixing container
low-tack masking tape
2" paintbrushes
clean, soft rags
2" hard bristle paintbrush
2" dragging brush

heritage kitchen cabinets

This traditional-looking country kitchen is actually a modern extension that was built to fit into the architecture of an early-19th-century farmhouse. The budget-conscious home-owners bought inexpensive stock kitchen cabinets, and I chose a vintage green paint and finish that would blend authentically with the rest of the country decor. Two simple techniques were used to decorate the cabinet doors; the centers were ragged and the sides were dragged. The white refrigerator, which stuck out unappealingly against all the deep colors, was camouflaged by an inset panel I finished to match the cabinets. (These panels are available for standard refrigerator and dishwasher doors.)

Many paint manufacturers today have a line of paint in traditional or heritage colors. These colors are limited to what was available in pioneer days when pigments or dyes were drawn from the farmland—grass, vegetables, berries, and earth. If you want to have a true country look, use these heritage colors inside and out.

INSTRUCTIONS

Prepare your surface following the instructions on page 14. You may find it easier to remove the doors from the cabinets and lay them on a flat surface to work, as we did here.

STEP 1: Remove the cabinet handles. Apply 2 coats of the base coat and let dry for 4 hours.

STEP 2: Work on one cabinet door at a time. Prepare the glaze. Mask off around the inside panel. Apply the glaze to the inside panel with a 2" brush.

STEP 3: Scrunch up a rag into a rose shape and dab it over the surface, removing some of the glaze and creating a mottled effect. Remove the tape and let dry.

STEP 4: To drag the outer edges of the door, mask off the inside vertical edge and apply a coat of the glaze. Pull a 2" hard-bristle, dry brush through the glaze, creating a dragged effect. Keep wiping excess from the bristles. Let dry completely. Mask off the outside of the horizontal edge and repeat the painting and dragging process.

PAINT AND TOOLS

Base coat
white latex paint, satin
paintbrush, small roller, paint tray

Painted finish
pencil, ruler
chalk line (optional)
¼" and 1" low-tack masking tape
light and dark cream latex paint, satin
2" paintbrush
mini-roller
varnish and brush

lattice backsplash

This kitchen was transformed into a bright, energetic space perfect for the young family who are renting the house. They wanted a quick fix without the cost of replacing the countertop and the series of unmatched cabinets. I basecoated the cabinets in a vivid peach color and colorwashed raspberry glaze over the top. A stencil border detail was created by using cream stencil paint and low-tack tape. The backsplash was plain white, so I painted an interesting lattice design across the surface. The combination of fresh paint and color is now what you see, not the out-of-date countertop and cabinets.

The lattice pattern is masked off in two stages in order to create a three-dimensional effect. There's lots of taping, but the area is small, so it goes quickly. Because it's a backsplash, I applied two coats of varnish for protection.

INSTRUCTIONS

Prepare your surface following the instructions on page 14. Apply 2 coats of the base coat and let dry for 4 hours.

STEP 1: Mark off a grid of diamonds using a chalkline or pencil; the one I've done here are 4¼" squares. I've included ¼" for the thin grout line.

STEP 2: Press the ¼" tape down firmly over the penciled grid lines.

STEP 3: With the light cream paint and 2" paintbrush, apply paint over the tape, extending about 1" on either side.

STEP 4: Remove the tape and let the paint dry thoroughly, about 4 hours.

STEP 5: Now apply the 1" low-tack tape over the center of the ¼" line.

STEP 6: With a roller, apply the dark cream paint over the entire surface.

STEP 7: Remove the tape and let the paint dry for 4 hours. You now have 2-toned lattice strips; the white ¼" base coat with pale cream on either side creating a 3-dimensional effect against the dark cream background. Apply 2 coats of varnish to the backsplash for protection.

twig cabinets

The owner of this old house wasn't ready for a complete renovation, but neither did she want to live with a shabby, dreary kitchen. We decided to have fun and create a rustic kitchen in a city home.

I gave the cabinet doors a fresh coat of cream paint. Because of their original condition—old paint drips, lumps, and bumps—it was impossible to make these doors look new, but applying lengths of willow in a simple pattern hid the imperfections. The twigs were first left to dry out, then nailed into place. I rubbed the cream base coat over the willow to highlight the texture of the wood. Thick twigs were used as handles to complete this makeover.

metallic diamonds

The backsplash in this 1950s-style kitchen was painted to coordinate with the faux-wood-grained cabinets on page 145. Diners were my inspiration here—lots of chrome and brushed steel. I've re-created this feeling with a traditional diamond pattern, using aluminum paint as a base coat.

I made a diamond template to fit the height of the backsplash, then marked around it with a pencil. I masked alternate diamonds, then brushed over them with aluminum paint that I tinted with blue. The alternating diamond colors simulate the effect of two-tone brushed steel.

INSTRUCTIONS

Prepare your surface following the instructions on page 14. Apply 2 coats of the aluminum base coat and let dry for 4 hours. If your pattern is not going to fill the backsplash, mask off the undecorated area to protect it.

STEP 1: Make a diamond-shaped template out of foam core or cardboard and draw a line down the middle. Using this line and a spirit level to make sure each diamond is straight, mark the shape of the diamonds along the backsplash by penciling around the template.

STEP 2: Mask off every other diamond with tape, making sure the tape crosses cleanly at the angles so the points will be sharp.

STEP 3: Prepare the glaze, one part each of blue and aluminum paints and 2 parts glazing liquid. With a foam brush that fits nicely into the corners, apply the glaze to the diamonds. Use a rough brushing movement so the glaze is lightly textured with brush strokes.

STEP 4: Remove the tape and let the glaze dry, then tape and paint the alternate diamonds in the same manner.

TIP: To protect the backsplash, seal it with 2 coats of varnish.

RECIPE

1 part latex paint
1 part water-based glazing liquid

PAINT AND TOOLS

Base coat
aluminum latex paint
sponge roller, brush, paint tray

Painted finish
low-tack masking tape
foam core or cardboard
pencil, ruler
spirit level
aluminum and blue latex paint
water-based glazing liquid
mixing containers
foam brush
varnish and brush

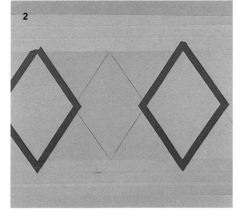
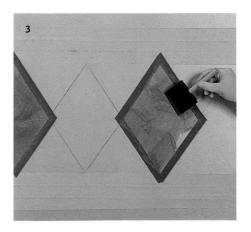

bathrooms

OPPOSITE: *The out-of-date tiles in this bathroom were given an imaginative makeover with the help of some paint and high-adhesion primer, applied before the surface was painted. The tiles were decorated with a rubber stamp with an African theme. In the shower area, four coats of varnish protect the finish from moisture.*

Bathrooms are one of my favorite areas to decorate. Because they are small and don't take long to paint, they are a good place to practice painted finishes on walls or ceilings. In older homes, the bathroom may have unattractive tilework that is too costly to replace, but the walls can be painted quickly and inexpensively.

Modern bathrooms have sparkling new tubs and sinks; however, this pristine atmosphere can also feel cold and sterile. Limited natural light is often a problem. The challenge in these small rooms is to give the eye something interesting, even fun, to look at. Painted finishes are perfect on the walls because the glaze used is durable enough to withstand moisture and fingerprints.

CREATE A DIVERSION

Until old bathroom fixtures can be replaced, you can minimize the dreary sight by drawing the eye to the walls. Although dark colors or large patterns are traditionally thought to make a room seem smaller, this is not always the case: In a bathroom, you can afford to be daring, even a little eccentric.

Painting ceilings is hard on the neck and back muscles. But working on a small bathroom ceiling won't tire you out, and it's a good spot for special effects.

Painted stucco will give an interesting textured finish to otherwise plain walls, and it holds up well under the wear and tear of daily bathroom use. Any of these special touches will minimize the presence of less than perfect fixtures and tiles and give you a way to add your own personal touches.

IMITATE EXPENSIVE MATERIALS

Special painted finishes can trick the eye and it's very gratifying to create a lush look that transforms a room at little cost. If you are going to paint faux marble or faux glass block, use realistic colors and shapes, and build the pattern on the wall as it would appear if you had used the natural materials. Several coats of color-wash will give warmth to a new bathroom by softening stark white walls.

TIPS FOR: *painting over tile*

Existing ceramic tiles are expensive to replace, and I'm constantly asked if you can paint over bathroom, kitchen, or floor tiles. You can paint on tile if you prepare the surface well and use the correct paint. However, even if you follow these instructions, painting on a ceramic floor will not stand up to heavy traffic.

A kitchen or bathroom backsplash can be given a whole new look, either by painting over existing tiles or adding tiles that you have painted to a plain wall.

1. *Painting over existing tile.*

   Clean tiles with a heavy-duty cleanser and sand to rough up the surface of the tiles. Apply a high-adhesion primer over the entire surface, including the grout lines. Use laminate, marine, or oil-based paint as a base coat. You can then stamp or stencil designs onto the tiles using oil-based paint.

2. *Painting loose tiles.*

   Porcelain or ceramic paint is water-based and designed to be applied directly over shiny surfaces such as ceramic tile, glass, china, and terra-cotta. You do not need to sand or prime the tile. It is thermo-hardening and requires time in your oven to set the color. Allow the paint to dry for 24 hours and then oven bake at 300–350 degrees Fahrenheit (150–160 degrees Centigrade).

3. *Inside a shower.*

   The best paint to use is epoxy paint or marine paint. Follow the manufacturer's instructions carefully.

RECIPE

1 part latex paint
1 part water-based glazing liquid

PAINT AND TOOLS

Base coat
turquoise latex paint, satin
roller, brush, paint tray

Painted finish
pencil, ruler
chalk line
aqua latex paint (or paler shade of
turquoise base coat), satin
water-based glazing liquid
mixing container
paint tray
small sponge roller
craft paper
stencil brush
small amount of gray and
white latex paint

Stencil
Mylar
marking pen
sharp knife
spray adhesive

faux glass blocks

New bathrooms can be luxurious because of their modern fixtures, clean lines, and fresh tiles, but they can feel stark and sterile. There is often no natural light in bathrooms in new homes, and a translucent glaze on the walls can help to open up the space.

I've always liked the look of glass blocks. They are often used by architects and designers to create the illusion of space and light. This small modern bathroom didn't have enough room for the real thing, so we replicated glass blocks with paint to achieve the same effect. I think it looks a lot more fun than the real thing.

Although the aqua color of the glass could look cold if it was painted as a uniform surface, using it as a painted finish in the blocks of glass gives it a wonderful transparent appearance.

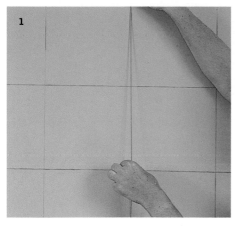

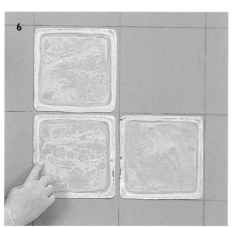

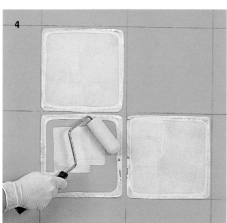

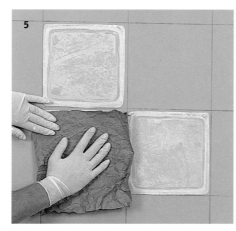

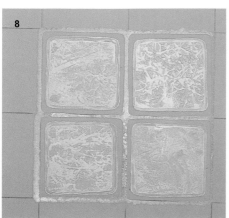

INSTRUCTIONS

Prepare your surface following the instructions on page 14. Apply 2 coats of the base coat and let dry for 4 hours.

STEP 1: Using a chalk line, make a grid over the base coat of 8¼" squares (8" blocks plus ¼" grout lines). For tips on measuring and mapping, see page 32.

STEP 2: Cut a block stencil from Mylar with the outer dimensions 8" square and the border sides ½" wide. Make the inside and outside corners slightly rounded. It's faster to make 3 or 4 stencils so you can paint 3 or 4 blocks at a time.

STEP 3: Line each stencil along the bottom and left block lines of the grid on the wall.

STEP 4: Prepare the glaze. Pour the glaze into the paint tray. With a small sponge roller, fill in the stencils with the glazes.

STEP 5: Scrunch up a piece of the craft paper, open it, and lay it over the glaze. Rub the paper with the palm of your hand, then remove the paper.

STEP 6: Rub your finger around the inside perimeter of the block to slightly smudge the paint.

STEP 7: With a stencil brush and a small amount of gray paint, stipple over the grout lines between the stencils.

STEP 8: Remove the stencils and repeat the process for the rest of the blocks.

RECIPE

2 parts latex paint
1 part water

PAINT AND TOOLS

Base coat
green latex paint, satin
roller, brush, paint tray

Painted finish
indigo latex paint, satin
mixing container
paper plate
sea sponge
paper towel

rental face-lift

Rental apartments often come with undersized, dingy bathrooms. Although landlords are not usually averse to tenants painting the walls, they won't allow alteration of the tiles. The best way to tackle this problem is to make the walls so interesting that the tiles disappear. In this small bathroom, we've sponged the walls in bright, contrasting colors, which also helps camouflage the original rough layer of paint.

A quick note about sponging, which is often the first painted finish that any of us attempt. It's easy to do: Just dab a sea sponge in paint, then press it loosely over a surface. But some thought is necessary to achieve a successful finished look. To keep the finish subtle, you should choose different tones of the same color. Or, if bright, contrasting colors are used, it's important to apply the sponge very carefully so that a uniform effect is achieved.

INSTRUCTIONS

Prepare your surface following the instructions on page 14. Apply 2 coats of the base coat and let dry for 4 hours.

STEP 1: Mix indigo paint with water and pour a small amount of the watered-down paint onto a plate. Moisten and wring out the sponge. Pick up some paint with the damp sponge and blot the excess onto a paper towel.

STEP 2: Apply the paint to the surface randomly with a light dabbing motion, turning the sponge periodically so the pattern differs. If the paint runs, there is too much water—add a little more paint. Keep going back over your work until the finish is fairly uniform. Cut a small piece of sponge to get into the corners of the room.

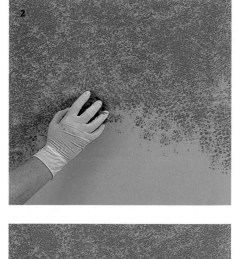

LEFT: *A bathroom identical to the one on page 160, in the same apartment building, has been given a whimsical effect by hand-painting baby blue swirls over a canary yellow base.*

stairways, doors, and fireplaces

The subjects of the following three chapters are the parts of the home that generally receive our attention only after we've completed the major and more compelling decorating projects. The ceilings have been painted, the walls decorated, and the floors have been fixed up, and now we can focus on the details. In fact, the stairways, doors, and fireplaces (if you have one) are an integral part of the overall design of your home. It's wise to think about how they will be treated along with the rest of the decor. Each of these elements has a special role to play in unifying the style of your home.

How you treat a stairway is determined mostly by its location and design. But you will also want to consider your home's character and whether you prefer carpet or paint. Carpeted stairs are a safe and quiet alternative to stained or painted wood, but there are times when a decorative finish is an irresistible and inexpensive alternative. Stairways are the link between floors, so use them to tie these areas together by repeating a color or a pattern on the steps and risers. All kinds of patterns can be created, whether freehand, stenciled, or stamped, or a variety of painted finishes can be applied. Painted stairs exemplify the cottage and country style; colorful faux runners and naive motifs are easy to produce, and they fit well into a casual lifestyle. But grander staircases can also be given their own unique look. And don't forget the staircase walls.

Doors are as much a part of your rooms' decor as the baseboards and window trim, and they often receive the same finish. But if your room is without detail, consider making the door a feature. Flat-faced doors are the perfect surface for creating painted fantasies such as trompe l'oeil moldings or stenciled designs. The finish needn't be complex to be effective.

A fireplace will be a focal point wherever it's located. But its design may not suit your taste. Building styles change with the times. Central heating and high-quality insulation have literally changed the face of today's fireplaces. Inserts are little more than a firebox that sits flush with the wall. New fireplace surrounds can be built at little cost with inexpensive wood and stock trim, and a coat of plaster or paint will finish the job. The solid presence of a faux stone or marble finish suits fireplaces perfectly.

I have chosen some of my favorite solutions for decorating these important features. They can be inspiring to work on and will prove to be the finishing touch to your beautiful painted home.

OPPOSITE: *This Victorian stairway was already a wonderful architectural element, but just by painting the risers with a simple stencil that mimics the design of the finial, we've made it even more interesting.*

stairways

Stairways are usually a prominent feature in a house because of their location and considerable use. According to the architecture and size of a particular home, stairway design varies considerably, from narrow and steep, winding up wall-hugging passageways, to the wide, sweeping steps of an elegant central staircase flanked by finely crafted spindles and newel posts. Although a stairway may not be the first area you choose to decorate, such a well-used area is worthy of attention, and it should carry on the decor you have established in the rest of your home. The style of the stairway can act as a link between rooms and floors.

Of all your household surfaces, probably the stairs must withstand the toughest punishment, so your decorating choice must be as durable as possible. Interior stairs are nearly always built with a good-grade hardwood. In some newly constructed houses, wall-to-wall carpeting may be laid over a poorer quality plywood that is not meant to be seen. In older homes, the stair carpet may hide dozens of nails that have been hammered into the steps to tighten loose and squeaky boards. So, if you decide to rip up the carpet, lift up a corner first to see what's there.

The walls in the staircase must be impervious to the plethora of fingerprints, dents, and scratches they will inevitably receive. This is an ideal area for a painted finish. The glaze will ensure that the wall is washable, and the broken paint will camouflage the marks. A bold combination of colors can open up a narrow stairwell.

A STEP IN THE RIGHT DIRECTION

Country houses, beach homes, and cottages are natural settings for paint and pattern on the stairs because of the constant tracking in of mud, dust, and sand. So are hot, humid climates, which do not lend themselves to wall-to-wall carpeting. We've become aware of the toxicity of particular glues and fibers in carpet, so painted stairs are an ideal decorating alternative if you suffer from allergies.

Staining and varnishing is the most durable solution, but if you want to add decoration and color, paint is a more interesting alternative. It's important to take into consideration how much use the staircase gets. Even with four coats of varnish for protection, the paint will eventually wear. However, if you choose certain designs such as country-style finishes, the wear and tear will only add to the look. For an elegant staircase, just paint side runners and leave the center stained.

RISE TO THE OCCASION

Another alternative is to paint and decorate the risers alone. This is a marvelous way to dress up a staircase, and it offers maximum visual impact. The risers get an occasional scuff, but any decoration will last much longer than on painted steps. Maintain the style you've created in the rooms or hallway around the staircase by choosing a pattern or a stencil that is compatible with your theme.

TIPS FOR: *painting staircases*

- Sand off old varnish and wipe clean.
- Paint the walls first. For hard-to-reach or high staircase walls, there are ladders designed specifically to sit safely on stairs. There are also extension poles for rollers and brushes. All can be rented.
- Paint the banisters and spindles next, then the risers, then the steps.
- Always start at the top of the staircase and work down.
- If the stairs must be used while you are working on them, mask off and paint every other step. When the first group of steps is completely dry, lay sheets of paper on them, then paint the final group of steps.
- Use at least 4 protective coats of varnish for painted steps and 2 coats for painted risers. Let the paint cure for a week before allowing shoes or heavy traffic in that area.

PAINT AND TOOLS

Base coat
white latex paint, semigloss
small roller, brush, paint tray

Painted finish
roller, paint tray
green latex paint, semigloss
low-tack tape
¼" artist's brush
bright primary colors (red, yellow,
blue, and white) of latex paint
low-tack varnish and brush

rag rug stairs

A narrow staircase in a Victorian cottage was given a new lease on life with the ingenious use of paint. This faux rug runner is so realistic that visitors are constantly bending down to touch it. The wood stairs, the baseboards, and the spindles and newel post were given fresh coats of semigloss white paint. A green runner was painted down the center of the staircase, then I chose bright colors and hand-painted irregular lines across the stairs. The pattern of colors was kept consistent, just as in a real woven rag rug. This marvelous effect creates the illusion that the stairway is much wider than it really is.

INSTRUCTIONS

Prepare your surface following the instructions on page 14. Apply 2 coats of base coat to the stairs and let dry for 4 hours.

STEP 1: With a roller, paint the green runner on the steps and risers using low-tack tape to keep the edges neat.

STEP 2: With an artist's brush, apply squiggly lines of primary colors across the runner, overlapping the edges onto the white about ¼". Alternate the colors to make a pattern similar in a woven rag rug. Let dry completely. Add 4 coats of varnish for protection.

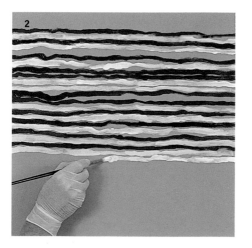

country staircase

This simple wooden staircase has been given a superb makeover by combing the treads and the risers. Combing is a casual country style perfectly suited to this cottage. As the paint eventually wears over many years the faded effect only becomes more fitting with the surroundings. Combing can be achieved with a professional rubber or metal comb used for wood graining, but here I used my own, cut from a piece of foam core.

I first basecoated the stairs in cream, and then combed each riser in horizontal stripes. Before starting the steps, I lightly stippled the lip of each step with the glaze. I combed a wiggly design onto the center of each step to give the effect of stair mats.

INSTRUCTIONS

Prepare your surface following the instructions on page 14.

STEP 1: Tape the edges of the stairs to protect the wall. Prepare the glaze. Make the comb from a piece of foam core cut with ¼" teeth. The comb should fit twice into the height of the riser.

STEP 2: Do the pattern one step at a time. I estimated the pattern, but you can measure it off with pencil marks at the lip if you like.

STEP 3: For the risers, apply the mustard glaze and pull the comb through the glaze horizontally across the top of the riser. Move down the riser and repeat. Wipe any build-up of paint on the comb onto a rag. Finish all the risers and let dry.

STEP 4: For the steps, apply the glaze to the step and lip.

STEP 5: Now pull the comb in straight horizontal lines across the step.

STEP 6: Then pull the comb in vertical squiggly lines down the central section of each step. Add 4 coats of varnish for protection.

RECIPE

1 part latex paint
1 part water-based glazing liquid

PAINT AND TOOLS

Base coat
cream latex paint, satin
3" paintbrush

Painted finish
mustard latex paint, satin
water-based glazing liquid
mixing container
pencil, ruler (if needed)
homemade foam core comb
newspaper
varnish and brush

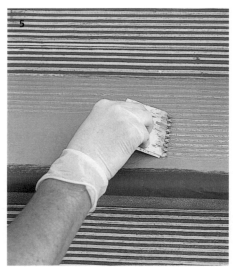
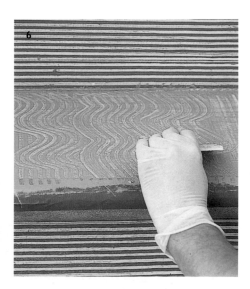

mexican staircase

PAINT AND TOOLS

Painted finish
kitchen sponge or upholstery foam
marking pen
pencil, ruler
Mylar
sharp knife
cream and any other color
stencil paint
paint tray
low-tack masking tape
or spray adhesive
stencil brush
paper towel
varnish and brush

If you're worried about wear and tear on painted stairs, a good solution is to paint just the risers. Although they do get kicked, they will last much longer than the treads, especially if they are protected with several coats of varnish. This was a rather drab wood staircase leading to a basement den. I sanded down the stairs and gave them an oak stain. Because the den was decorated in a Mexican style, I stenciled the risers to imitate handmade Mexican tiles. The fabulous effect fools guests into thinking that they are real tiles. The background of the faux tile is just a stamped square of cream paint. Stencils were cut from Mylar and applied over the cream squares using authentic Mexican colors.

INSTRUCTIONS

Prepare your surface following the instructions on page 14.

STEP 1: Cut the kitchen sponge into 4" squares. Pour a small amount of cream paint into the paint tray. Dip the sponge into the paint and blot off the excess; the surface should be saturated to achieve an opaque background. Press the sponge into position on the riser. If the imprint has too many sponge holes, turn the sponge around and reapply. Let dry for 4 hours.

STEP 2: Choose a favorite tile; trace the pattern onto the Mylar and cut out the stencil. Complicated tile designs require more than one stencil (overlays). Add registration marks and label the top and bottom of each stencil.

STEP 3: Use tape or spray adhesive to position the stencil on the cream background. Dip the end of the stencil brush into the paint, remove the excess on a paper towel, and fill in the stencil. Reposition the stencil on each remaining tile and fill it in. Let dry, then add 2 coats of varnish for protection.

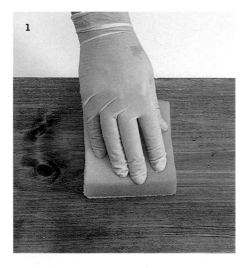

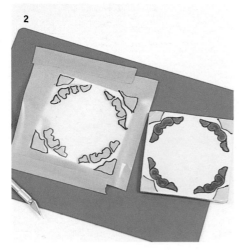

dotty stairs

This modern wood staircase leads to a children's playroom in the basement. I wanted the stairs to be as cheerful as the plastered walls (see page 60). The stairs were first sanded down, then given a coat of primer and two base coats of apple green paint. To decorate the steps I took a foam roller and cut out a variety of different shapes with a knife—tiny hearts, squares, triangles, and dots. I then rolled the roller through a tray of primrose yellow paint and rolled it over the steps. Although this is a fast and easy finish, it only works in strips of no more than 5' long, as the color will begin to fade as the roller runs out of paint. This effect is ideal for a dado border or even on furniture.

PAINT AND TOOLS

Base coat
apple green latex paint, satin

Painted finish
8" or 12" sponge rollers to fit your space
sharp knife
primose yellow latex paint
paint tray
varnish and brush

INSTRUCTIONS

Prepare your surface following the instructions on page 14. Apply 2 coats of the base coat and let dry for 4 hours.

STEP 1: Cut or pull out small, differently shaped pieces from the sponge roller. They can be circles, triangles, or squares.

STEP 2: Pull the roller through the yellow paint until the roller, but not the holes, is saturated. Roll it over the green surface in one smooth stroke, pressing hard.

STEP 3: Use the 1" brush to fill in any missed spaces, such as where the risers meet the steps. Let dry, then apply 4 coats of varnish.

NOTE: Here I found it easier to just roll the pattern onto the center of the steps, leaving a green border.

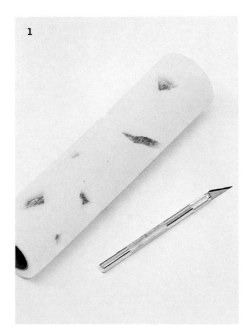

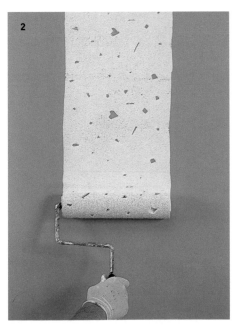

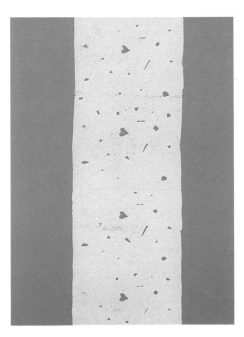

doors

Take a moment to count the number of doors you have in your house or apartment. Include the exterior doors, the doors leading to the basement or attic or balcony, the bedroom closet, linen closet, and storage closet doors, and the doors between rooms. In a small apartment or an open-plan design, you may have as few as seven or eight doors. The average three-bedroom house has as many as twenty doors. That's a lot of doors to think about. Their presence is a force to be reckoned with, because they are very much a part of your home's decor.

The decision is whether to diminish their worth or make them a feature. There are no set rules, but here are two important guidelines I use when deciding how to treat doors: I look at the style and condition of the doors and where they are located. The flat-fronted swing doors on the opposite page have been given a classic touch by reproducing the beautiful domed shape of the plant stand. A stencil was cut to size and the design was stenciled directly onto the door.

WORK WITH THE AGE AND STYLE OF THE DOOR

If you live in an older home, chances are good that your doors are made of solid wood and are decorated with carved or raised moldings or even scrollwork. These beautiful doors need no further embellishment,

LEFT: *My heart missed a beat when I came across this bohemian painted metal door at Jake's Hotel in Jamaica. The faded, color-washed stucco walls and vibrant delphinium blue door would inspire anyone to play with color.*

OPPOSITE: *In this*
bedroom, these
central doors belong
to a built-in closet.
While the walls were
colorwashed in
apricot and ocher,
the doors were each
painted a different
shade of green, then
stamped with a
diamond pattern
using the alternate
green. The trim is
highlighted with
red, gold, and blue.

and I would leave them alone or return them to their natural state, or simply give them a couple of coats of semigloss paint.

Old doors with layers and layers of paint are a big job to make perfect. They can be stripped and then repainted, but often chemical strippers destroy the glues, and the doors never hang quite right again. By using a simple painted finish such as dragging, you can disguise an uneven surface.

Expensive architectural details such as carved doors are used less frequently with each passing decade; most interior doors are now hollow and either plain-faced or have grooves and graining pressed into them. Plain, or flat-faced doors provide the easiest surface for a painted finish, offering a virtually blank canvas to play with. Pressed wood doors aren't suited to most faux finishes because of the grooved grain lines. To make these doors more interesting, you can rub in paint to highlight the grain and panels. Louvered doors are the most difficult to decorate and are generally left white or painted the same color as the walls.

CHOOSE TO BLEND IN
OR HIGHLIGHT THE DOORS

The location of the door will give you some idea of how to treat it. If there are a number of doors visible from one space, such as a hallway, it's best to treat them all the same. In fact, all doors opening onto a hallway, upstairs and downstairs, look better when they match.

An excellent way to incorporate doors into a room's decorative scheme is to continue a wall finish onto the door. This will make the breaks less obvious as well as dress up a bland door face.

If one or two doors stand alone, you might make them a special feature. This is an excellent place to experiment with faux finishes that may be intimidating on a grander scale.

Bedrooms can be almost overpowered by doors, especially if they are all located on the same wall. First, look at their style, then decide which doors would be best diminished and which would make an attractive feature. Closet doors are usually your best bet to highlight. Incorporate some of the colors or patterns from your bedding or curtain fabric onto these doors.

TIPS FOR:
painting a paneled door

1. Remove any hardware. Sand away any loose or cracking paint and dried paint drips; it is not necessary to sand all the way down to the raw wood.

2. Repair any cracks or splits with wood filler or caulk.

3. Apply a coat of primer over raw wood or any repairs.

4. Order of painting: Start with the panels. Load paintbrush, apply paint to the center of the top panel, and brush the paint up and down so that paint won't build up around the edge or molding grooves. Brush vertically, then horizontally across the panel until the paint coat is smooth. Work from the top of the door down, and when all the panels are painted, paint the horizontal and vertical strips that surround the panels. Brush strokes should move in the same direction as the wood grain. Paint the door frame last.

5. Two base coats are recommended. Sand between coats for a smooth finish.

trompe l'oeil paneled door

The interior doors in most new homes have little detail. A white painted door in a decorated room can look like the front of a refrigerator, but its flatness actually makes it a perfect surface to paint. Either finish the door in the same manner as your walls, or use this surface to create an interesting feature.

Trompe l'oeil is French for trick the eye. It is one of the most fascinating art forms because it is not only artistic, but also usually amusing. Although much trompe l'oeil work requires artistic talent, this faux paneled door is simple to create. With just a pencil, a ruler, masking tape, and paint, you can make a flat-fronted door look as though it has recessed panels.

INSTRUCTIONS

Prepare your surface following the instructions on page 14.

STEP 1: Apply 2 coats of the base coat and let dry for 4 hours.

STEP 2: Mask off the 5 panels, leaving a 1" gap between the tape; it will become the faux molding. Use a spirit level to make sure the panels are straight.

STEP 3: For this trompe l'oeil effect, we are imagining that the light is coming in from the top right, so the top and right molding strips will be dark and the bottom and left molding strips will be light. To create this illusion, miter the corners by placing pieces of tape diagonally across the top left and bottom right corners of each panel's "molding," creating an upside down _L_. Paint the top and right strips with 1 or 2 coats of dark gray. When all the gray is painted, remove the pieces of diagonal tape and let dry.

STEP 4: This time place tape on the mitered corners, leaving the lower and left molding clear, and paint these molding strips light gray. Remove all the tape and the illusion will appear.

PAINT AND TOOLS

Base coat
medium blue latex paint, satin
roller, brush, paint tray

Painted finish
¾" low-tack masking tape
pencil, ruler
spirit level
dark and very pale gray
latex paint, satin
1" paintbrush

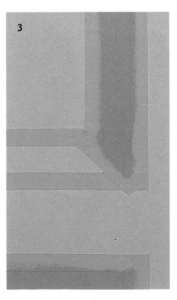

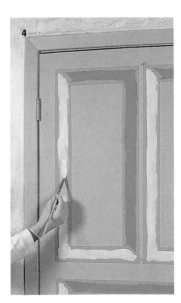

RECIPE

1 part latex paint
1 part water-based glazing liquid

PAINT AND TOOLS

Base coat
buttercup yellow latex paint,
satin finish

Painted finish
green, pink and blue latex paint, satin
water-based glazing liquid
mixing containers
low-tack masking tape (optional)
homemade comb or rubber comb
bottle cork
pencil with tip eraser
hard-bristle paintbrush
2″ paintbrush
artist's brush

crazy kids' door

Doors in children's rooms can easily become part of the decor, whether you're painting a mural, stenciling a frieze, or just adding color. In this young girl's room, I chose apple green walls and a palette of four eye-catching colors for the border, trim, and door. Simple patterns were created with a variety of tools found around the house: a cork, a homemade comb, a paintbrush, and a pencil eraser. The baseboard and trim around the door were first given a base coat of two coats of white paint. The walls were masked off with sheets of newspaper, then the children were given the four colors, long-handled ½-inch brushes, and large smocks. The children splattered the paint over the trim with squeals of delight. The door was given a base coat of buttercup yellow, then the four panels were decorated with different patterns. The door was such a success with my little friends that I carried on the design around the room as a lively border.

INSTRUCTIONS

Prepare your surface following the instructions on page 14. Apply 2 coats of the base coat and let dry for 4 hours.

STEP 1: Prepare the glazes. Mask off the door panels if you wish.

STEP 2: Combed panel: Apply the pink glaze to the inside of the panel, covering 100% of the surface. To make the design, pull the comb through the glaze while it is wet, horizontally and then vertically.

STEP 3: Polka-dot panel: Apply the green paint to the panel and let dry. Dip a cork into the blue paint and press randomly over the panel. I added a little yellow dot to the center of each blue dot using the eraser end of a pencil.

STEP 4: Striped panel: Pull a hard-bristle paintbrush with blue glaze over the panel to create stripes.

STEP 5: Waves and dots panel: Using the pink paint and an artist's brush, paint wavy lines with dots between the waves.

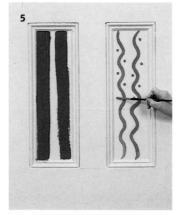

fireplaces

Ever since fire was discovered, the hearth has been a central gathering place for man to feel safe and warm, to cook, to tell stories, and to relax. Technology changed many of these rituals; homes were built with central heating systems, and we cooked our meals at the kitchen stove. The fireplace was no longer a necessity. With the advent of central heating, many fireplaces, thought to be drafty and a waste of precious interior wall space, were plugged up or removed. But we discovered that we missed the ambience of an open hearth, the crackle and glow of the flames, the feeling of comfort. Today, a fireplace remains a top selling point for most of us whether we are renting or buying a home.

If you have a fireplace, whether or not it is functional, it is usually the focal point of the room. Depending on the age and style of your house, the fireplace surround could be built of stone, brick, plaster, or wood. It may be large and imposing or, as is the case with many modern dwellings, a pared-down version, almost nonexistent. The challenge is to make this natural focal point fit in with the rest of your home. If the surround is in poor repair, unattractive, or underdone, what are the options for decorating this important feature, for maximizing its inherent appeal?

Bricks are a common building material for fireplace surrounds and interior chimneys. Over time the mortar between the bricks will dry, loosen, and partly chip away. The brick face will collect dirt, soot, and grease. To restore the brick, remove any dirt and loose mortar with a steel brush, and remove stains with a cleaning compound. Repoint the bricks with mortar tinted to match what's there. If you are still unhappy with the look of the bricks, they can be painted, but remember they will still look like bricks. Flat latex paint looks best, because bricks are not glossy by nature.

If the brickwork is unattractive or not your taste, the entire surround can be refaced and restyled with plaster or drywall. A variety of faux finishes can be applied to the new flat surface.

WOOD MANTELS AND FIREPLACE SURROUNDS

Many older fireplaces were enhanced with beautiful, hand-carved wood panels and mantels. The wood may have deteriorated, or perhaps it wasn't top quality and was meant to be painted. Here's a perfect opportunity to use elegant painted finishes such as faux marble, lead, and stone. In the Victorian era, faux finishes were often used on wood surrounds. The wealthy had the real thing, but others had painted copies of elaborate stone or wood. Nowadays, these faux finishes have become a precious addition to the home.

ADDING OR DECORATING A NEW FIREPLACE

For convenience and cost, zero-clearance fireplaces are being installed in new houses and apartments. There is little decoration to them; the firebox simply fits into the drywall. Instead of making the firebox the focal point of the room, why not decorate the surrounding chimney or wall in a special finish to draw the eye to a more pleasing surface? A popular alternative is to build out a face with medium-density fiberboard (MDF) or plywood and strips of molding. The fiberboard is easy to cut and has a smooth surface, perfect for painting. You don't need to use fire-resistant paint as long as you're not applying it to the inside of the fireplace. Varnish need be applied only to the top of the mantel to protect it from scratches.

OPPOSITE: *I dressed up this flat-fronted brick fireplace with a large piece of architectural molding I had rubbed with brown glaze. It makes a splendid mantel.*

RECIPE

1 part latex paint
1 part water-based glazing liquid

PAINT AND TOOLS

Base coat
white latex paint, satin
roller, brush, paint tray

Painted finish
pencil, ruler
¼" low-tack masking tape
level
dark and light sand and
white latex paint, satin
water-based glazing liquid
mixing containers
3 mini-rollers
clean, soft rags
clear plastic wrap
small amount of terra-cotta
latex paint, satin
¼" artists' brush

faux limestone

As decorating styles changed over the years, often the original mantels in older homes were removed, as was the case in this living room. The fireplace surround had then been squared off with drywall, leaving a boxy shape quite unfit for such a beautiful room. To begin the transformation, I replaced the brick hearth with tumbled limestone slabs, a stunning pale stone in natural hues of beige, cream, and white. The stone pieces are tumbled in a machine that softens the edges and dulls the finish. I added a curved mantel made of fiberboard to the top of the surround.

The flat surfaces of the fiberboard mantel and surround are perfect to paint. Here, I copied the colors and textures of the real limestone on the hearth in a stone-blocking finish that complements the pale frescoed walls.

INSTRUCTIONS

Prepare your surface following the instructions on page 14. Apply 2 coats of the base coat and let dry for 4 hours.

STEP 1: With the tape, mask off the limestone blocks, which are slightly irregular rectangles. Use the spirit level to make sure they are straight. This will be the color of the grout.

STEP 2: Prepare the glazes. Work on several blocks at a time. With a small roller, apply the dark sand glaze horizontally.

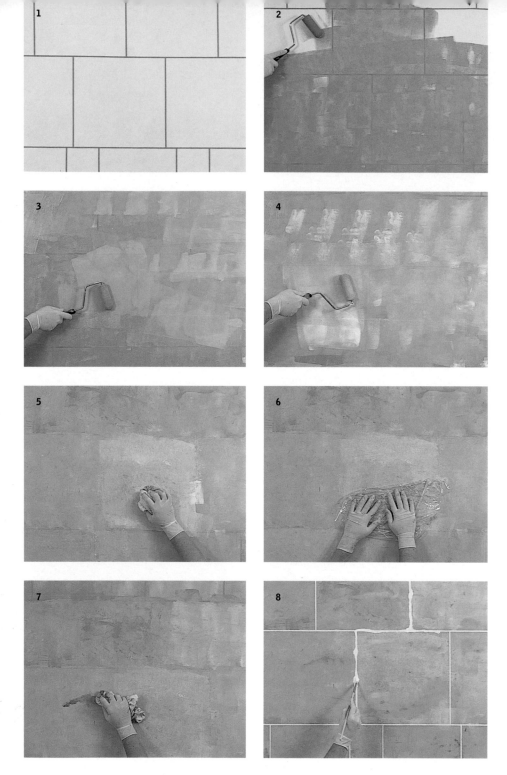

mexican tile fireplace

This imitation adobe fireplace was an elaborate solution to a common decorating problem. The original surround was painted brick, and the only way to disguise brick is to either drywall over the top (see faux limestone, page 183) or, as I have done here, plaster over the bricks. I chose a handful of colorful Mexican tiles and glued them randomly onto the bricks. The whole area was then plastered level with the tiles. The white plaster was left unpainted in keeping with the style of real adobe walls. Now, the fireplace enriches this cozy Mexican-style family room.

STEP 3: Apply the light sand glaze with another roller horizontally over the same blocks.

STEP 4: Repeat with the white glaze and another roller. This roller will start blending the colors together.

STEP 5: With a rag, blend the colors over each block.

STEP 6: Fold a piece of plastic wrap, accordian style, then open it. Press it over each block to create tiny creases. They will be different for each block.

STEP 7: With a soft rag, dab a small amount of terra-cotta paint sparingly over some of the blocks to create the markings found on real limestone.

STEP 8: Remove the tape and let dry. With an artists' brush, paint over the grout lines with pure white paint to soften the corners and make the lines slightly irregular and more authentic looking.